Solitary

Alone We Are Nothing

Gladys Ambort

☒ WATERSIDE PRESS

Solitary Alone We Are Nothing
Gladys Ambort

ISBN 978-1-909976-61-0 (Paperback)
ISBN 978-1-910979-63-1 (Epub ebook)
ISBN 978-1-910979-64-8 (Adobe ebook)

Copyright © 2018 This work is the copyright of Gladys Ambort. All intellectual property and associated rights are hereby asserted and reserved by the author in full compliance with UK, European and international law. No part of this book may be copied, reproduced, stored in any retrieval system or transmitted in any form or by any means, including in hard copy or via the internet, without the prior written permission of the publishers to whom all English language rights have been assigned worldwide.

Cover design © 2018 Waterside Press by www.gibgob.com Front cover photo of the author as a young girl, Luis Plantón; back cover photo of Gladys Ambort today, Arielle Masson.

Printed by Lightning Source.

Main UK distributor Gardners Books, 1 Whittle Drive, Eastbourne, East Sussex, BN23 6QH. Tel: +44 (0)1323 521777; sales@gardners.com; www.gardners.com

North American distribution Ingram Book Company, One Ingram Blvd, La Vergne, TN 37086, USA. Tel: (+1) 615 793 5000; inquiry@ingramcontent.com

Cataloguing-In-Publication Data A catalogue record for this book can be obtained from the British Library.

e-book *Solitary: Alone We Are Nothing* is available as an ebook and also to subscribers of Ebrary, Ebsco, Myilibrary and Dawsonera.

This first English translation and edition published 2018 by
Waterside Press Ltd
Sherfield Gables
Sherfield on Loddon, Hook
Hampshire RG27 0JG.

Telephone +44(0)1256 882250
Online catalogue WatersidePress.co.uk
Email enquiries@watersidepress.co.uk

TABLE OF CONTENTS

Acknowledgements *iv*
About the author *v*
Dedication *vii*
For the Memory, for Justice, for a Dream *ix*

Prologue: Arrival in Paris..13

Introduction: For Freedom of Expression..................................17

    PART 1: **My Prisons**... 35

    PART 2: **Solitary Confinement**...111

    PART 3: **Desolation**...135

    PART 4: **My Release, Exile …**..167

Epilogue: Never Again...183

Forty Years Later …..187

Index *189*

ACKNOWLEDGEMENTS

I am indebted to Julie May, English teacher at Ifage,[1] Geneva, for reading and correcting the translation into English that I did of the French version of this book, published in 2010. Thanks for her generous work, her patience, and encouragement.

I am very grateful to Peter Forbes, tutor on the Narrative Non-Fiction course at City, University of London, for his careful revision of the English text and his assistance, and Susan Harrison for her contributions based on comparisons between the Spanish and the English versions of parts of this book, as well as for the support she and her husband, Steven Nickless, have given me.

My gratitude to Nicola Padfield, Master of Fitzwilliam College, University of Cambridge, and her husband, Christopher Padfield, a former chair of England and Wales' national Association of Members of Independent Monitoring Boards, whose kind recommendation led to the opportunity of being published by Waterside Press.

Many thanks to Bryan Gibson, director at Waterside Press, a lawyer turned publisher, without whose valuable advice this book would not have reached readers' hands in such a refined form.

For his photos of Córdoba Prison I must thank Lucas Crisafulli of the University Programme at the Prison, Faculty of Philosophy and Humanities, National University of Córdoba.

Finally, my gratitude to readers for sharing this narrative which, although not recent, remains a universal story. It could happen anywhere, at any time, and unfortunately it still does.

Gladys Ambort
Geneva, July 2018

---

1. *Fondation Pour la Formation des Adultes à Genève*: see www.ifage.ch

ABOUT THE AUTHOR

Gladys Ambort is a resident of Geneva. According to the author, "Living has been her most successful undertaking", and she is happy to have reached 60-years-of-age. After obtaining a PhD in Humanities from Geneva University, she writes, lectures in colleges and universities, works with the languages she has learnt… and rides her bike.

To my son Alexander who was only a boy when the French edition of this book was published and has since become a fine young man.

FOR THE MEMORY, FOR JUSTICE, FOR A DREAM[2]

> Of so many deaths, give me the memory,
> of all those who became ash,
> of a generation, give me the memory,
> their last fury, their last pain.
>
> Isaïe Spiegel, *Give Me the Memory*[3]

To the memory of the political prisoners of the Penitentiary of the San Martín district of Córdoba, Argentina shot between 1976 and 1978, and through them, the 30,000 people missing in that country who disappeared during the military dictatorship. So that it never, ever, happens again, either in Argentina or anywhere else.

Eduardo Daniel Bártoli
Gleam Ricardo Verón
Miguel Ángel Mozé
José Alberto Svagusa
Eduardo Alberto Hernández
Ricardo Alberto Yung
Diana Beatriz Fidelman
José Ángel Pucheta
Miguel Ángel Barrera
Esther María Barberis

---

2. Title of a booklet published in Córdoba in 1999 by relatives, friends and survivors, in memory of those mentioned in the text above and overleaf.
3. Isaïe Spiegel, *"Donnez-moi la Mémoire"*, in *Anthologie de la Poésie Yiddish: Le Miroir d'un Peuple*, Paris, Gallimard, 1987, p.441, translated by the author.

José Cristian Funes
José René Moukarzel
Miguel Hugo Vaca Narvaja Jr
Higinio Arnaldo Toranzo
Gustavo Adolfo De Breuil
Ricardo Daniel Tramontini
Carlos Alberto Sgandurra
Claudio Aníbal Zorrilla
Mirta Abdón
Marta Rossetti de Arqueola
Raúl Augusto Bauducco
Liliana Páez
Florencio Esteban Díaz
Jorge Oscar García
Miguel Ángel Ceballos
Pablo Alberto Balustra
Oscar Hugo Hubert
Marta Juana González de Baronetto
Osvaldo De Benedetti

Justice is in accordance to History,
It varies from case to case
And depends on power.
Justness instead
Can only be found
Within oneself
And does not vary.

Gladys Ambort

Gladys Ambort.
Photo: Arielle Masson.

PROLOGUE

Arrival in Paris

[...] Loneliness is not standing on the dock, at dawn, looking at the water avidly. Loneliness is not being able to say it because you cannot get around it because you cannot give it a face because you cannot make it synonymous with a landscape. Loneliness would be this broken melody of my phrases.

Alejandra Pizarnik, "The Word of Desire", The Musical Hell[1]

---

1. *Collected Works*, Buenos Aires, Corregidor, 1999, p.157, translated by the author.

Solitary

Prologue

> I was twenty. I will not allow anyone to tell me
> that youth is the best time of life.
> Paul Nizan, *Aden Arabia*[2]

From 1974 onwards, Argentina experienced years of terror following the struggle between leftist movements and guerrillas, on the one hand, and extreme right nationalist factions, on the other. The supposedly democratic government led by María Estela Martínez de Perón encouraged repression by police and paramilitary groups of the entire Argentinean left, and, more broadly, all progressive forces in the country. This climate of terror led to the establishing of a military dictatorship, the bloodiest Argentina had ever known. Thousands of people disappeared, others were imprisoned. Being a student at college and an activist in a leftist party, I was imprisoned for almost three years. Subsequently expelled from my own country, when I arrived in France, I was not yet twenty-years-old.

She is nineteen-years-old; she has a child's face. She does not want to give her name for fear of reprisals that the military might take vis-à-vis her family. These words appeared in the Parisian newspaper *Le Matin*; they were written about me. Still confused by fear, I learnt French by reading them. They referred to my participation in a press conference which the committee for refugees, CIMADE,[3] had organized for me. On this occasion, I was seated next to the legendary French philosopher Simone de Beauvoir,[4] barely aware that this was a great event. After a group of French lawyers had spoken about their trip to Argentina as part of their activities in support of human rights, I tried to testify about what I had just lived through.

---

2. Paris, Maspero, Cahiers Libres, n.8, 1960 [1932], p.65, translated by the author.
3. *Comité Inter Mouvements Auprès des Evacués. Service Oecuménique d'Entraide.* The CIMADE is a committee which has been supporting, first evacuated people, afterwards refugees, now the undocumented. It helps people who, for political or economic reasons, are forced to abandon their own country.
4. In 1949, Simone de Beauvoir published *The Second Sex*, in which she foreboded the feminist revolution. It remains to this day a central text in the investigation of women's social oppression and liberation.

Solitary

That day in February 1978, in front of many journalists and other listeners, I spoke about my experience in prison without a clear awareness of what I was saying. I told my story and tried to report everything that was happening in Argentina, about imprisonment and abductions. I talked about the cold, hunger and disease; about punishment and isolation. Hood and handcuffs, solitary confinement and gaolers, cell and wing, torture and pain, disappearance and terror; all these words made up my first speech in the language of Molière. I explained methods of detention, security and visiting systems, periods of total isolation. I described sanctions and abuse, transfers to concentration camps and assassinations. I spoke about our comrades, those who were still in prison, those who no longer existed and those whose fate was unknown. But nothing of what I said that day expressed what I had really gone through.

I did not understand the meaning of my words very well. They certainly did not convey the pain which churned in my stomach at that moment. The cold of that February marked the first of all those winters I was to endure in Paris, not having chosen my destiny, trying to comprehend what I was saying at the press conference that day to those journalists who saw on me a child's face.

INTRODUCTION
FOR FREEDOM OF EXPRESSION

Solitary

Córdoba Prison.
Photo: Lucas Crisafulli.

Introduction

I

I had arrived in France on January 9th 1978 after being held in three different prisons in Argentina for nearly three years. I was born and grew up in the city of Córdoba, but I had been arrested in Río Cuarto, a smaller city in the same province of Córdoba, shortly after celebrating my seventeenth birthday. My political awakening had occurred at the age of fifteen, on September 11th 1973, when I attended a huge event in the city centre to protest against a *coup d'état* instigated and supported by the USA's Central Intelligence Agency (CIA) in Chile, which had resulted in the assassination of President Salvador Allende.

At the time, I was a student at the Manuel Belgrano College of Commerce. Subsequently, following a strong current of politicisation of Argentinean youth, I became an activist in a left-wing political party called *Vanguardia Comunista*.[1] I continued to participate in popular and student mobilisations and advocated a new economic and social order which, at the time, seemed wholly clear and easily achievable. I belonged to a generation that did not accept the world as it stood and had decided with others, to change it. We wanted to proclaim a new truth, different from that which prevailed at that time. Embracing Marx's theories, we believed that history had a predetermined course, which would inevitably lead to Communism, where all kinds of oppression and exploitation would finally disappear, and we wanted to accelerate the process. Also, our generation had been born around 1955, the year that the Argentinean Air Force bombed civilians on the Plaza de Mayo in Buenos Aires, flagrantly demonstrating their disdain for human life.

Along with my political awakening in a left-wing party, I rejected many of the values on which I had based my identity until then, those I had inherited from my family and my community, as well as those I had formed with my peers. Dissatisfied with the society in which I lived, unhappy to see so much poverty and inequality, I joined those who did not want to resign themselves to the development model we

---

1. Communist Vanguard.

were being promised, and I refused to wait for the course of history that would bring about our future. Along with many others, I defended the idea that the social order in which we lived did not correspond to any natural order, so that we should change it. Convinced of the justness of our ideals, I wanted to be an interpreter of this transformation and to play an active role. However Swiss or German my ancestors were, I was born in Argentina and I felt I totally belonged there. Argentina and its inhabitants were part of my identity, and I rejected the then widespread idea that poverty and general underdevelopment were due to laziness and cowardice. I joined those who believed that only the ownership of the fruits of their labours by those who produced them would improve the situation, abolish injustice and oppression, and finally entitle everybody in the world to work, food, freedom and wellbeing.

My boyfriend was active in the same political party as I was, and his leaders had decided to send him to Río Cuarto to develop political awareness in rural areas. Río Cuarto is located two hundred kilometres from Córdoba, the capital of the province. Thus, I decided to go and settle down with him after completing my fourth year at high school. Given my age, I could not do this without the consent of my parents, so I decided to get married. In this new city, I enrolled at the National College of Commerce where I continued to study while developing my militant activities. These mainly consisted of distributing newspapers containing a different political and economic stance, even antagonistic, to the official position.

Until the day I was denounced by one of my professors. She did it on the basis of a comment I had made in a history class about the war in South Vietnam, where, in April 1975, the National Liberation Front aided by the North Vietnamese Popular Army had vanquished the US Army. I had claimed that if the smaller army had defeated the world's largest, most powerful one, it was because it fought for freedom and ideals. The professor did not appreciate this interpretation one jot. In the middle of the Cold War, it left no doubt about my sympathy for the Eastern or Communist Bloc. She reported this to the college principal who informed the police. Following this, in May 1975, two months after I had started at the new college, my husband and I were arrested.

II

> Freedom, Sancho, is one of the most precious gifts heaven has given humankind; neither the treasures hidden on earth nor those covered by the sea can equal it; for freedom, as well as for honour, one can and has to venture life, and on the contrary, captivity is the worst evil that can befall us.
>
> Miguel de Cervantes, *Don Quixote de la Mancha*[2]

Being a minor emancipated by marriage made my imprisonment possible. As an opponent of the political regime, a member of a left-wing party and an activist in college, at seventeen-years-old I was regarded as a danger to State security.

"She is a lioness", the judge commented about me. Fortunately, the law does not depend on the fantasies of a judicial functionary. The two lawyers in charge of defending my husband and I had no difficulty in proving that none of my political activities contravened constitutional rights enjoyed by every citizen: namely of expressing their disagreement with the government and advocating the establishment of another, more appropriate, regime. Despite this, the federal judge of the court at Río Cuarto decided to extend our custody, alleging that we had violated Article 2, sections (a) and (c) of the National Security Act.[3] This special law had been approved in September 1974 by the government of María Estela Martínez de Perón to criminalise and punish those who "for achieving the goal of their ideological beliefs, would try or advocate by any means, to alter or suppress the institutional order and the social peace of the Nation". This law did not concern, in principle, Communist activities

---

2. Madrid, Anaya, 1999, translated by the author.
3. These provisions of National Security Law (20.840) rendered liable to two to six years' imprisonment those who carried out "acts of release, propaganda or dissemination intended to indoctrinate or promote behaviour that could affect or disrupt the institutional order and social peace of the nation" and "those who possess, produce, print, publish, reproduce, distribute or provide material which propagates communications or images related to such behaviour".

in themselves, except in cases where they were carried out in opposition "to ways approved by the National Constitution and by the laws that organize the political, economic and social life of the Nation".

When our lawyers submitted our case to the Federal Court of Appeals for Córdoba, they invoked this provision to indicate that our preventive custody lacked any merit. It was obvious, in their eyes, that although the propaganda material found in our house reflected unambiguously our political ideals, mere possession of it was not a criminal offence. But despite this argument, the federal judge considered that reading such material allowed one to hold an obvious intention to disturb the institutional order and social peace. In response to such perspicacity on the part of the judge, one of our defence lawyers, a young woman of twenty-five-years-of-age, using a kind of irony still tolerated at the time, argued that "despite the fact that the material found at the defendants' home and [that] the political organization they belonged to was permitted by the repressive legislative penalties in force, they were victims of the 'in-built prejudices' of the judge". In the text presented to the appeal court, our lawyer indicated that it was "extremely dangerous for the maintenance of democracy and the protection of individual rights", to extend without foundation, the list of literature envisaged by law 20.840 so as to condemn its possession. This departure constituted prosecution for one's convictions. "The resolution of the judge of the trial court contradicted the lawfulness of the organization responsible for publication and its newspaper".

The decrees which had restricted the freedom of the press affecting many newspapers and other media did not concern the publication, its circulation and, still less, the possession of the materials found at our home. The items found were shown on a detailed list which accompanied the counts in the indictment as follows:

- a book *Selected Works of Mao Zedong*;
- a book *Neocapitalism and Mass Communication*;
- a book *The Imperialist Domination in Argentina*;
- a book *The Red Orchestra*;
- a book on Trotskyism;
- a *Third-World* magazine;

- seven copies of *El Riocuartense* magazine, newspaper of the local committee of *Vanguardia Comunista*;
- two copies of *Rebel Youth* magazine;
- two copies of the Student Centre newspaper of the Manuel Belgrano College;
- one copy of *Brown List, Young Students* magazine;
- seven copies of *No Transar* (No Compromise), the *Vanguardia Comunista* newspaper;
- one copy of *New Time* magazine, the Argentinean Revolutionary Communist Party's newspaper;
- one copy of *Revolutionary Subjects* magazine;
- one copy of *Beijing Informs* and several other printed papers, as well as a file containing a collection of *No Compromise*, the *Vanguardia Comunista* Central Committee's magazine.

೧೨

As for me, in addition to the possession of these various books, newspapers and magazines which were regarded as subversive, I was charged with the offence of "indoctrination" for distributing copies of *El Riocuartense* magazine to teachers and students who were my classmates at college. In particular, I had given a copy of this magazine to my political economics professor, and I had suggested that the article on secondary students published on page 12 of that magazine be debated in class. After reading the article, he underlined to the class the Communist spirit of the magazine in which the article had been published, but also said that it was not fair to condemn whoever thought differently out of hand.

When he was called as a witness before the judge he stated that I had given him this magazine believing it to be lawful. He added that I had proposed that a discussion be held on the subject, because I wished it to be sensibly debated in the light of the different ideologies which existed in the world. My classmates, for their part, declared that I used to discuss all sorts of topics with the professors with a thorough knowledge of what was at issue and with a much higher level of analysis than other students. Furthermore, in advancing my appeal, my lawyer pointed out that the vice-principal and other members of the teaching staff had declared that I was a very good student, that I showed great interest in gaining knowledge and in developing various issues. She underlined that, previously, at the Manuel Belgrano College, the active participation of students in the learning process was of fundamental importance and that the free discussion of topics, including political ones, was permitted. Consequently, she concluded, it was unacceptable that such a practice could be considered criminal and held against me: "Based on these principles, the defendant expressed openly her opinions before her professors and classmates. Also, the defence argues for the protection of these principles, considering that calling them into question would mean infringing the basic right to academic freedom in general." The inequity of the accusations against us, our lawyer finally argued, was the more obvious "if we take into account that the student Gladys Ambort is only seventeen-years-old".

With this, she expected that the appeal court would quash the trial judge's violation of our right of opinion. Thanks to this intervention and after a process which lasted for over five months, our case was temporarily closed. It was one of the last to be tried in accordance with legal requirements of due process. Some time later, when our other lawyer, Elías Semán, disappeared after being arrested, that requirement was rescinded, giving way to criminal arbitrariness.

Elías was one of the founders of *Vanguardia Comunista*, a party, whose existence, as our young lawyer pointed out during our appeal, was authorised by the national constitution. An attorney on labour matters and defender of political prisoners, Elías was also a writer. At the time of his disappearance, he was helping the activists Carlos Altamirano, Ricardo Piglia and Beatriz Sarlo to found the cultural magazine *Point of View*. Nobody could, or was allowed, to defend him and no trial was held of the charges against him. He disappeared along with dozens of other comrades within the extermination camp of *El Vesubio* in the province of Buenos Aires, which was under the control of the First Corps of the Army, then led by General Carlos Guillermo Suárez Mason. Elías Semán is one of the long list of missing persons never seen or heard of again.

III

> To be one thing or another, we need the consent of society. But when society disowns what we were in days gone by, we never were it.
>
> Jean Améry, *Beyond Crime and Punishment*[4]

After the Federal Court of Appeal recognised that there were no criminal charges to merit our incarceration, my husband was released on condition of his good behaviour. Unlike me. I had to stay in prison under an order of the National Executive Power (NEP). According to a decree implemented some days after our arrest, the State was entitled to hold us without having to justify why we represented a danger to the security of the nation. This prerogative, thanks to which the State could arrest, with or without reason, anyone considered dangerous, existed after María Estela Martínez de Perón, the head of the Government, imposed a state of emergency in November 1974, suppressing all individual rights. Although our cases were identical, the order applied to my husband was rescinded some time before. I never knew why.[5]

The injustice I fell victim to from that moment onwards demonstrated the willingness of the NEP to act against anyone who manifested opposition to it, its principles or its values. My incarceration was a manifestation of this will expressed by a section of society that intended to silence opposition or eliminate opponents so that they would never express themselves again. Although the authoritarian, illegal power exerted by civilians and the military in Argentina dated back several decades, it had never acquired the monstrous dimensions which started with the first assassinations and imprisonments in 1974, and which led to the military *coup d'état* of 1976. Military forces besieged the State apparatus and triggered a wave of violence such as the country had never known

---

4. *Par-delà le Crime et le Châtiment, Essai Pour Surmonter l'Insurmontable*, Paris, Actes Sud, Collection Babel, 1995, p.34, translated by the author.
5. The NEP signed a different decree for every single citizen they wanted to keep in prison.

before. A study by Prudencio García,[6] a colonel in the Spanish Army, highlighted that, in its design, Argentinean officers' training had been strongly influenced by strategies applied by the French Army in Indochina and Algeria, namely the systematic use of torture. Trainees had also received instruction in some military centres in the USA.

With the support of large sections of Argentinean civil society, the military tried to eradicate every thought and action that could threaten their absolute power. To maintain their status and privileges, they definitively silenced many of those who claimed the right to have their voices heard. Those they could not kill, either openly or in the shadows, were locked away in prisons or concentration camps, in spaces especially designed to physically or morally annihilate opponents, *to make them disappear.*

Unlike so many other Argentineans and youngsters of my generation, I was not eliminated from the world but set aside. To prevent me from trying to change this world, I was locked-up and denied any action at all. After three years in prison and confinement, I found myself in Paris, far from my family and my country. During the press conference organized by the CIMADE in February 1978 mentioned in the *Prologue*, I felt helpless; I could not remember my college, or having been a good student, let alone the subjects which, according to my classmates, I discussed with great ease. What remained of my knowledge after all that time in prison, and what use was it if I could not understand what I felt at that moment? I hardly had the strength to wonder what my cellmates would have thought had they known I was seated next to Simone de Beauvoir, the philosopher who had so much contributed to women's emancipation.

---

6. In Hugo Vezzeti, *Pasado y Presente, Guerra, Dictadura y Sociedad en la Argentina*, Buenos Aires, Siglo XXI, 2002, p.74.

IV

> [...] Imagine now a man who is deprived of everyone he loves, and at the same time of his house, his habits, his clothes, in short, of everything he possesses: he will be a hollow man, reduced to suffering and needs, forgetful of dignity and restraint, for he who loses all often easily loses himself [...]
>
> Primo Levi, *If This is a Man*[7]

I had been released from prison on January 8th 1978, the day before my arrival in Paris. I had asked the military junta for permission to leave Argentina. Of the two punishments on offer, imprisonment or exile, I had chosen the latter.

Officials of the federal police came to pick me up at Devoto Prison early in the morning and took me first to their headquarters, then to Ezeiza International Airport in the province of Buenos Aires. Late in the afternoon, prior to accompanying me to the plane, they allowed me to see my family who had been waiting all day in the room next to mine to say their farewells. I was flying abroad at a time when international travel was far rarer than it is today. The idea of crossing the ocean was strange to me, and that of one day returning to my country close to fiction. However, I was so exhausted that I did not have the energy to feel any emotion whatsoever. My sisters gave me bags and other objects that I held without paying much attention. What I did notice instead were the head and arms of Julieta, my beautiful rag doll, jutting out from one of the bags. It was one of the presents I had received for my fifteenth birthday, just two years before being imprisoned.

The police officers took off the handcuffs that I had worn the whole day, for me to be able to hug my mother, my brother, my sisters and a dear friend who had managed to reach this place, but they did not release

---
7. London, The Orion Press, 1960, p.21, translated by Stuart Wolf from *Se Questo è Un Uomo*, 1958.

Solitary

me until I boarded the plane. Along with my passport, I was handed over to Air France boarding staff. Passing the passport to me, one of them informed me that I was on French soil, and that therefore I was free. But at that moment, this meant merely a change of legal status for me. Seated in the back row, by the window, when the plane took off the condensation from the air conditioning dripped on my head. During the flight, the drops continued falling constantly. The man seated next to me called the steward; I would not have dared. I felt as though I was still in prison. A decree had allowed me to be released and travel abroad, but it had not sufficed to liberate my spirit.

During that press conference in Paris, I had a tumult of things jostling together in my mind, but in no way the feeling of freedom. Moreover, nothing of what I said allowed me to truly understand what I felt. I did not succeed in making my words coincide with what I had really experienced. Despite my rudimentary knowledge of French, it was not a linguistic problem. I felt deprived of any language as such. My experience of life, the way in which I had grown up and formed my character, did not offer me the tools to express what I felt. I knew there was something inside me, but I was not able to identify it. None of the tools acquired until then to grasp reality, to capture and understand the world and its phenomena, no language known or shared with others, allowed me to express what was happening in my spirit at that moment. Nothing, absolutely nothing was as before, and even if I had been a polyglot I would not have succeeded in explaining that I did not feel myself anymore.

How to explain to all those journalists who thought I was a child, that I was actually... nothing? How to explain that one has lost oneself, even if for the others, one seemed to be present? I was standing on my feet; I was alive, young and free. Regaining the sixteen kilos I had lost during my incarceration was only a matter of time. Afterwards, as my boss said many years later when I was working in a bank in Switzerland, I had to turn the page. However, he was Jewish; he should have known that, when we try to forget the past, we are condemned to repeat it.[8]

---

8. Per the thoughts of the poet and philosopher George Santayana, which can be read at Dachau Concentration Camp: "Those who cannot remember the past are condemned to repeat it".

Introduction

V

> Then for the first time we became aware that our language lacks
> words to express this offence, the demolition of a man.
> Primo Levi, *If This is a Man* [9]

My three years in prison had been long and difficult. Now that I was free, nothing was as before. Quite definitely, I was not the same, and neither was the world I saw around me. During the years that followed, what had happened to me in prison was beyond my comprehension, and I therefore felt powerless to explain it. After undergoing great trials, after suffering traumatic hardships, when one tries to transmit things to others it is almost impossible to describe what one feels deep within oneself. It is likely that the words to do that do not exist, or if they do they have not been put in an order which would allow us to explain what has happened, since this does not belong to what we normally perceive and to what we refer to through everyday forms of expression. The result of the experience then, is painful. It exists, but it cannot be put into words. The feelings are trapped and try to find other ways of expression, because it is almost impossible to describe the moral suffering which, despite its unbearable nature, has no visible signs or specific location. These feelings are so elusive and imperceptible; they are so indefinable that the body often ends up manifesting a physical pain to finally be able to express them.

Confronted by this limitation of language and the impossibility of putting some order into my confusion, suffering occupied my whole body and prevented me from living normally. If not feeling one's body is a symptom of welfare, because in this state the body is an immediate prolongation of our desires and intentions, I felt my body as something completely apart from myself. If stomach ache oppressed me almost

---

9. P.21.

permanently, I often had the impression that my whole body was paralysed; it was as if it had stopped functioning. I felt completely disjointed, as if I had, not a body, but a heap of fragments with not a link between any of them. It was as if I had to drag something dislocated, a bag of pain, in which it was impossible to identify each part and feel who I was.

During my stay in prison, I felt the pressing need to talk. I expressed this desire often in my letters to my sisters. I wanted to pour out my heart, to talk about all I was experiencing. In the situation of isolation in which I was, there was nobody I could share my impressions and my feelings with, and I needed to tell them what I was accumulating within me. But once outside the prison, each time I intended to speak, tears systematically replaced all narrative. During my youth I cried as I would never have imagined it was possible to cry. Then I learnt that there is no more powerful medicine than tears, which, shed without being repressed, show us the exact dimensions of our suffering, which we hardly admit and recognise otherwise.

Afterwards, I tried to create an image. On the one hand, I *drew* an oval with my finger in the air, as though I had wanted to re-energise an imaginary circuit which had stopped working within me. On the other, I *showed* how something had broken inside me, and I drew, either in the air, or across my chest, a sloping line, in the shape of a saw. But the mental images do not always offer the precision required by speech, and therefore I failed to accompany the image by uttering anything at all. It was not a straight line that would have defined in a clear and neat way what had broken, but a dislocated line, and therefore, much more difficult to repair. One can think of the skin or any other material: a single piece divided by a straight tear might be sewn, glued or joined back together with ease. The mark, the scar, the trace of what happened remains, but the part of the person or object can be made functional again. In the case of a cut in the shape of a flash of lightning, as I imagined instead, it is difficult to make the two parts fit again. And if small fragments have disappeared at the time of the rupture, one will never be able to join them up again.

VI

[…] in this cell, something was broken inside me.
Gladys Ambort, in *Listening-in to the Silence*[10]

In 1992, some years after I moved to Geneva, members of the International Committee of the Red Cross based in this city contacted me for an interview about my life in prison. They wanted to make a documentary with several testimonies on the detention conditions in prisons in countries as diverse as Argentina, Kosovo, Gabon and Cape Verde. Joëlle Comé, who was responsible for the report, drew the conclusion that conditions of imprisonment and methods of torture used throughout the world were all similar. This reinforced my idea that the testimony of my experience in prison did not add anything to what had already been written in recent history, what was known to the general public, or at least to those who did not need to deny reality to justify their existence or their wellbeing.

Most Argentineans, for instance, did not want to be informed. They tried to deny all evidence of the surrounding reality, or they declared that what had happened to us was not a coincidence. "It's no wonder it happened," they would say when they heard of the fate that was reserved for us, as if, somehow, we deserved it. Therefore, if I had the opportunity to tell them about my ordeal, it was only to reopen my wounds and confirm my helplessness, my isolation and my feelings of loneliness. Despite the certainty that their attitude was false, despite the belief that their responses were motivated by cowardice imprinted by an ideology shared by much of the population, some cracks remained in me through which a feeling of guilt infiltrated. As often happens to the victims of violence and abuse, I had internalised the legitimacy assumed by those who had tortured us.

---

10. In Joëlle Comé, *À L'Ecoute du Silence*, Geneva, ICRC, 1993, translated by the author.

As for people abroad, in the late-1970s, they knew that, in Argentina, a football player worked miracles, that the countryside was extensive, and that people ate the most delicious beef in the world. But they did not necessarily know that repression and extermination of political opponents was rife in prisons and concentration camps located near Buenos Aires, then one of the greatest cities in Latin America. They did not know that people were confined, humiliated, tortured and frequently killed. But apart from informing them of the horrors a dictatorial power can perpetrate, I thought that no account would allow me to explain what I felt and turn it into knowledge.

The day I was filmed for the ICRC documentary, however, not only did I speak about what I had experienced in prison but I also cried. Given my inability to explain my tears, I wanted to apologise. But I was only able to say that, in prison, *something had broken inside me*. For me, this expression meant a spiritual rupture, chaos, mental disorder and deep pain, but I could not explain this reality to anyone. Almost ten years later, during the autumn of 2001, Christine Ferrier, the documentary producer at the ICRC, contacted me again. Sometime before, the two professors who were directing my doctoral dissertation on domestic power relations at the University of Geneva, had encouraged me to work on my experiences as a prisoner in Argentina. My first reaction was to refuse, thinking that I would be unable to do it. But they disagreed. From their position of authority, they managed to persuade me to consider what I had previously never been capable of undertaking.

While I was trying to get used to the idea of writing about experiences I had almost given up on understanding and was gradually discovering the philosophical and psychological concepts that might explain what had happened to me, identifying the words with which I could name what hurt me so much, Christine Ferrier, who had been responsible for the production of the documentary, contacted me again because she wanted to ask my permission to use my voice. Her colleagues at the ICRC were assembling a permanent exhibition at the International Museum of the Red Cross in Geneva, and they wanted to re-use my voice when, during our interview ten years earlier, I said that *something had broken inside me*. Then I became aware that Christine, Joëlle and their colleagues, who had visited so many prisoners throughout the world, had realised, long before I did, what it was that had happened to me: when somebody is left alone in captivity, something inside them can break.

This rupture occurred in February 1977, two years after my arrest. I had been placed in solitary confinement for fifteen days for having allegedly scratched the small table in the visiting room where I had received a visit from my sister. During these fifteen days, there was an irremediable rupture after which my life changed fundamentally.

But it is only now that I am able to sketch out some ideas and organize this story about my prison experience and about what I felt in the punishment cell. I do not intend to recount in detail everything I experienced in prison. Each event was of course important, but I want to concentrate on this rupture I was exposed to, by being completely isolated. From this event, I explore the two years in prison preceding it, in search of the experiences which might explain the condition in which I was when I was put in solitary confinement.

Solitary

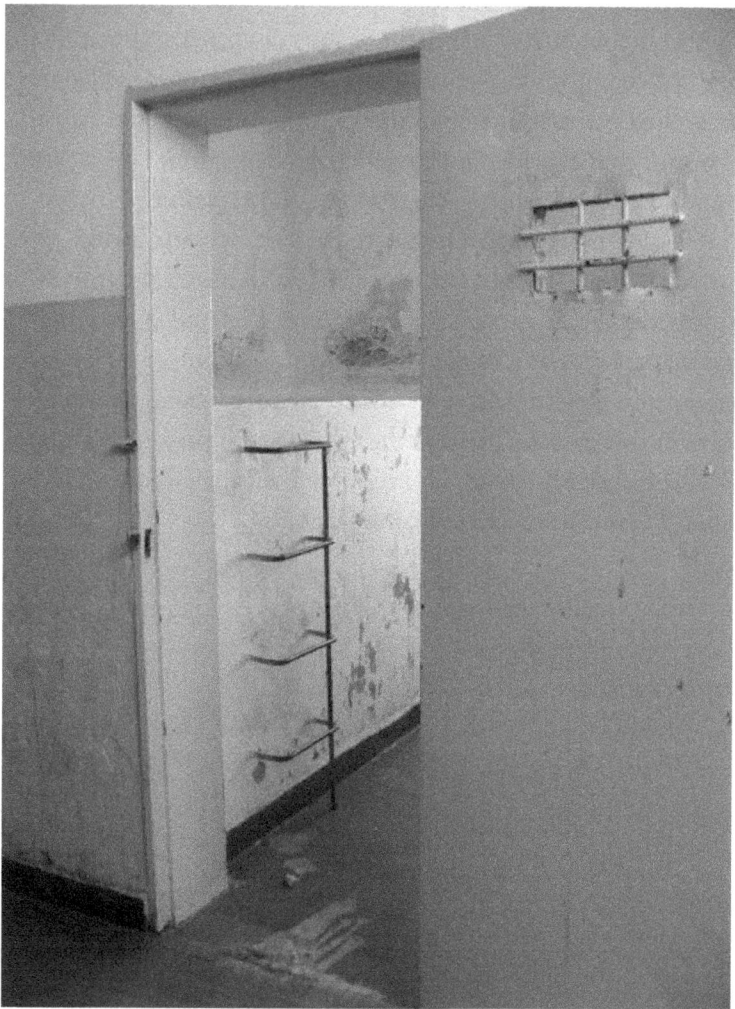

My cell in Córdoba Prison. This shows the concrete space where the mattress was laid, and the stairs I sat on top of to talk to my neighbour through a small light window on the top of the wall. The bars on the opening in the door did not exist when I was there. The small window was and has always remained unframed and a potential hazard.

PART ONE
MY PRISONS

> I relate here what I lived through. The horror in it is not gigantic.
> At Gandersheim there was no gas chamber, no crematorium.
> The horror there was darkness, absolute lack of any kind of
> landmark, solitude, unending oppression, slow annihilation.
>
> Robert Antelme, *The Human Race*[1]

---

1. Vermont, USA, The Marlboro Press, 1992, p.5, translated by Jeffrey Haight and Annie Mahler from *La Race Humaine,* 1957.

Solitary

The windows of our cells in Córdoba Prison. The projecting windows of the first floor, where I was held, hide a concrete slab below the window where we could sit, as can be seen in the picture on page 64, and as described on page 85.

Photo: Lucas Crisafulli.

VII

> I have gradually seen the light as to the most universal deficiency in our kind of cultivation and education: no one learns, no one strives after, no one teaches—the endurance of solitude.
>
> Friedrich Nietzsche, *Daybreak: Thoughts on the Prejudices of Morality*[2]

> [...] there, in the ultimate depth of all the rest, and from this same place, we never feel completely alone. We know that other people like us exist [...] Loosing this awareness of being analogous to others, of being a unity in an environment where there are others like us, drives us to madness.
>
> María Zambrano, *Persona y Democracia*[3]

In her study of Nazism and totalitarian regimes, the German philosopher Hannah Arendt[4] distinguishes between isolation and loneliness. She associates the first with the political life of a community and the second with human life in its entirety. Terror "can rule absolutely only men who are isolated against each other [...]," writes Arendt. In Argentina, the terror started indeed as a process of isolation of individuals, with measures banning assembly, association and organizing. Being the beginning of terror, isolation is "its most fertile ground; and always its result." Terror can act only if people are isolated because, by isolating them, it deprives them of all power. Isolation creates powerlessness, since power, according to the author, can only be exercised through the concerted actions with others.

We can be isolated from others without, however, being alone, says Arendt. But we can feel very lonely in a situation where we feel abandoned

---

2. Cambridge University Press, 1997, Book V, §443, p.188, translated by R J Hollingdale from *Morgenröthe*, 1881.
3. Madrid, Ed. Siruela, 1987 [1958], p.26, translated by the author.
4. *The Origins of Totalitarianism*, New York, Harcourt Brace & Company, 1979 [1948], pp.474–477.

by all human companionship, without however being isolated from the others.

Those who wanted to impose terror in Argentina arrested me on May 27th 1975, when María Estela Martínez de Perón ruled the country. The police came to arrest me at home and locked me in a cell, alone, at their headquarters. In this phase, my links with the outside remained intact. I did not feel abandoned and my psychological integrity at that moment was not threatened. Although I had been put aside from society and isolated in a cell, I still retained the memories of my loved ones and felt myself to be in contact with them in my mind.

Feeling the presence of my husband, imprisoned in a neighbouring cell, was also of fundamental importance. From the first moment we were locked-up, we started calling each other by whistling. Although we had been subjected to separate and solitary confinement, and that it was the first time we were exposed to such torture, knowing that we were still near each other was reassuring and comforting. In a certain way, it meant that the isolation was not complete. We were still able to keep some contact between us. When the initial three-day period of total confinement, during which I was kept lying on the floor in that small cell, came to an end, my door was left open and I was allowed to go outside and walk down the corridor. I managed to climb up to the bars of a window from where I could see the courtyard below. When my husband was allowed to leave his own cell, I was able to see him. The rest of the time, we continued to communicate by whistling. For that, we used a series of codes that we created spontaneously. We emitted a long sound to let each other know that we were still there, particularly early in the morning when we started a new day. That was followed by a more musical sound intended as a greeting. It meant we were happy to hear from each other. We were even able to intonate question marks. We wanted to know if each of us in our cell was doing fine.

Furthermore, at police headquarters, prostitutes were constantly coming and going and I could talk to them. I also knew that, sooner or later, my family would learn where we were and, in fact, it was one of the prostitutes who, once released, phoned my sisters to inform them what had happened to us.

Days passed. We were living in very bad conditions. We were cold and ate poorly. One day, my husband, who still had some money in his pockets, gave some of it to one of the policemen for him to bring us food from a nearby shop. It seemed obvious that it was not fresh, since I was terribly sick quite soon after eating it. Forced to lie on the floor, I suffered from a severe bout of dysentery. I was so dehydrated that after only a few days I had lost more than ten pounds. My physical condition deteriorated to such a point that I had to be taken to see a doctor. His diagnosis was blindingly clear: this girl, he said, is simply suffering from confinement.

But despite the deterioration of my physical condition, I did not allow myself to be overcome by despair. Unlike isolation, loneliness "is closely connected with uprootedness and superfluousness […]," says Hannah Arendt. "To be uprooted means to have no place in the world, recognized and guaranteed by others; to be superfluous means not to belong to the world at all." None of this happened to me. I also held in me the presence, strongly idealised, of those who fought for a better world. Indeed, in my mind I created an ideal image of my comrades. The fact of being isolated not only confirmed my sense of my position among them and in the world, but also gave deeper meaning to the struggle to which I had committed myself, and it afforded me more recognition from those of my companions who were still active outside. In a certain way, a direct confrontation with those who represented our enemy contributed to strengthening our unity, and with it my notion of belonging, upon which, in the words of Arendt, depends "the experience of the materially and sensually given world…". The fact that we find or feel ourselves to be in touch with other people, "regulates and controls all other senses…". If we do not share this sense of community, "each of us would be enclosed in his own particular sense of data which in themselves are unreliable and treacherous." Only because we have a community spirit, that is, only because not one person, but people in the plural, inhabit the earth, can we trust our immediate sensual experience.

In establishing this sense of community which helps us to exist, dialogue plays a fundamental role. But it can be just in the mind. Even when we are all alone, we can create dialogue in our heads by remembering others, with how we think the others might respond to our thoughts. Thinking about others prevents us from being completely alone. We can interact with the memory we have of them. This is how it felt to me. I found answers to my concerns and to the questions I asked myself through my mental communication with other people. I *knew* why I was where I was, I *knew* who it was who had imprisoned me and what they represented, I *understood* the reasons for my existence. The image of those whose presence I felt with particular intensity within me kept me from all existential questioning. In my opinion, the motives for my incarceration were entirely justified. The college professor who had denounced me to the police knew that I would be isolated, not only from my classmates, but also from my community. Besides, nobody had reacted to her gesture. But I had the support of all my fellow party members with whom I fought for a new society in which, we were convinced, this type of mind-set would exist no more.

Also Hannah Arendt emphasises the ability of a person to develop mental dialogue. In addition to the difference she makes between isolation and loneliness, that author, based on the writings of Epictetus, an emancipated Greek slave who became a philosopher, makes a distinction between loneliness and a solitary life. "Loneliness," says Arendt, "is not solitary life. Solitary life requires being alone..." And when we are alone, we can be together with ourselves, and therefore we do not necessarily suffer from a state of loneliness. "In solitude..." writes Epictetus, "I am 'by myself' together with my self, and therefore two-in-one, whereas in loneliness, I am actually one, deserted by all others." Strictly speaking, every thought is elaborated in solitary life, between me and myself, says Arendt, "but this dialogue of the two-in-one does not lose contact with the world of my fellow-men because they are represented in the self with whom I lead the dialogue of thought". To live in society, we need to be one again, and that is why solitary life should not be prolonged.

VIII

> Prison has two lives. One is locked in the cells, sternly
> isolated from the entire world — and yet related to the world
> in the closest bonds in the case of political prisoners.
> Julius Fucik, *Notes from the Gallows*[5]

Thanks to the diagnosis of my physical condition established by the doctor, in early June 1975 we were transferred, my husband to the men's prison in Río Cuarto, and I to the Convent of the Congregation of *Bon Pasteur* which served as a prison for women. I was sad to be separated from him, but getting out of the police van, the image of my oldest sister waiting for me near the entrance to the convent reassured me. It did not surprise me. It was as if in my life everything had returned to normal. She had responded to the call of the prostitute, caught the bus and come to see me. I do not know if the latter was aware of the importance of her gesture, so simple but so fundamental to us.

For more than six months, I stayed in this prison, where the women under arrest were looked after by nuns. Although I suffered from separation from my family, my friends and my comrades in the party, thanks to the countless gestures of support I received from them, I felt their company and I had their presence inside me. I could not share my feelings with them daily, nor go on with my usual activities, but my morale continued to remain high. I did not lose my memory of the outside world or of all those with whom I had grown up. I undertook manual, intellectual and physical activities from morning to evening, and I even learnt how to play the guitar, something I could not have done before, due to the meagre resources of my family. Here, one of the nuns was happy to teach me how to play some simple folk melodies. In late July, two months after my arrest, this is what I wrote to my mother:

---
5. New York, New Century Publishers, 1947, p.47.

> [...] this may seem surprising to you, but I find my days short. I do many activities. Among them, I work, I read, I do embroidery, I knit and I write. In any case, everything I carry out shows very well that you are always with me and that I feel next to you all.
>
> How great it is all I learn here. These are not big inventions, or exceptional subjects, but I learn them with great determination and much joy. Moreover, I try to read a lot in order to learn and elaborate new ideas and opinions.

I especially regretted not to be able to continue with my studies, but I did my mathematics or chemistry revision convinced that I would go back to college soon. I particularly remember that I spent hours reading the manual of organic chemistry and how I marvelled when I discovered the lesson relating to bread-making. It taught me how to make food I had only been able to buy until then. It appeared as magic to me. It was like discovering the hidden secret of things.

In another letter, I wrote as follows:

> I feel very, very well. I transform each day into a productive day, full of interest and joy. Actually, everything is beautiful.
>
> I hope you'll come to visit me as soon as you can. But if you cannot, please know that I do not get bored. I do not feel sad for being alone either. On the contrary, I do twice as many activities as usual, so that the affection I have for you becomes productive instead of being reduced to abstract words.

I added that I did the same in relation to my husband, whom I could see every Thursday when I was taken to his own prison:

> I try to do many things during the week in order to give them to him on Thursday. It wouldn't be fine if I spent the whole week saying that I miss him without doing anything to show that the love we feel for each other is something concrete, something which results in constructive things.

I often dreamt about being a mother, and then I felt particularly happy to take along with me the trousseau I was preparing with the handiwork teacher. The latter had taught me how to make babies' vests, to cut and sew the hems of bibs and to embroider motifs in cross-stitch. I also learnt to knit small jackets, jumpers and sleep suits. I became a specialist in knitting bootees, with the seam outside so they would not hurt the delicate skin of the baby's feet. However, the teacher had to remind me that I had to make bigger clothes than I was doing, because, she said, they were meant to dress a baby and not a doll.

Furthermore, although I could not enjoy the regular presence of my loved ones, I was not completely alone. My relationship with the prison authorities was excellent. The nuns allowed my family and my friends to visit me anytime and stay for as long as they wanted to. Although such generosity, as my mother explained to me one day laying her finger on her cheek, was motivated by their preference for white people and our Swiss and German origins, it was nonetheless an advantage for my psychological and physical wellbeing. This preferential treatment allowed me, more than once, to enjoy an unexpected visit from one or other of my sisters. I was surprised by their whistling to let me know that they had arrived. They had borrowed the sound codes that my husband and I had invented during our solitary confinement at police headquarters to communicate with each other.

Luisa, a thirty-seven-year-old guard, had become my friend. Her company was very important for me, so that the days when she was on duty and those on which she was not were quite different. Luisa protected me and, perhaps for the same racial reasons as the nuns, granted me relatively privileged treatment compared to other inmates. Obviously, this made me feel uncomfortable. If I was in prison, it was because I refused any kind of favouritism in relation to others. Luisa, on the contrary, was very pragmatic and careful. She made me eat at her table, seated on a small stool she reserved exclusively for me. It was probably thanks to her precautions that I did not catch syphilis. Indeed, all the women who came to *Bon Pasteur* suffered from this disease, as confirmed by the blood tests carried out periodically.

But the husband of Luisa's niece was a police agent, and that also bothered me. She spoke often about him. The "police forces" in Argentina embodied repression and corruption. A leftist militant could therefore not appreciate a police officer, whoever he was. But even that did not prevent me from building a quite affectionate relationship with Luisa. We talked at length and we did it with a confidence and a depth that only increased with time.

Among the nuns, Mother Clementina, small and elderly, showed her affection for me in many different ways. Whenever she left the convent refectory after lunch, she passed under my window hiding from the others, called to me softly and offered me part of her dessert, which she had hidden under her habit, and which she could not eat due to her diabetes. Mother Gabriela, a plump woman, but much younger and active, made me smile. She came every evening to my room to try to convert me to her Catholic faith. On the one hand, she claimed the importance of each individual on earth by saying that even the thinnest hair cast a shadow on the ground. But on the other she asserted that all delinquents must be put up against a wall and shot!

And then there was also my friend Elisa, a young girl of fifteen with dark skin and short frizzy hair. As she was always smiling, her beautiful teeth illuminated her complexion. Outside of prison, she had practised prostitution and was detained in the section adjacent to ours, reserved for the young girls placed under the mandate of the juvenile court. Since she had been in *Bon Pasteur* for a long time, she enjoyed the privilege of moving around the building freely. The nuns entrusted her with many tasks that allowed her to come and go from her section to ours. We developed a nice relationship. She admired me devotedly. As soon as she saw me, her round face brightened. But one day, the nuns found her reading a story for adolescents I had lent to her. They certainly judged that this literature did not respect their religious teachings and forbade her from any contact with me. Passing under my window, she told me in tears that she no longer had permission to come to see me.

But the main factor that helped to keep me in good spirits during the first months of my imprisonment was the relationship I maintained with my husband who was in the other prison. At that time, we felt great affection and respect for one another. Every day we wrote countless pages filled with stories of ordinary life, ideals, dreams and love. We exchanged our letters on Thursday each week when the police came to fetch me and took me to see him in his prison. For four hours then, I enjoyed the pleasant atmosphere created by all the parents who came to visit political prisoners. We were also able to spend time alone together in his cell and share a relationship that, despite our imprisonment, was fresh, healthy and full of joy and satisfaction.

In a letter to my family, I said that one Thursday when I went to see my husband, I had been very happy. I explained that he had prepared a delicious snack, that we had played with a ball and that we had felt wonderfully well:

> Each day we love each other a little bit more. This situation, instead of making our relationship more difficult, has consolidated it still more. Since our visit on Thursdays is not long enough for us to talk about everything we think, feel or do, we tell all this by letter. Apart from all these beautiful things we tell each other, we exchange critical comments and opinions. This allows us to continue advancing as a couple, as individuals and as revolutionaries.

Far from renouncing our ideals, indeed our being in prison only strengthened them. Although the regime of terror expanded its grip on the population, intending to isolate us more and more, I managed to keep a clear, strong mind and above all to keep hope alive. Shortly after our arrest, extreme right-wing paramilitary groups, which at the time were wreaking havoc in the city, bombed our house, causing extensive damage. They wrote murderous threats on the walls. The construction of the house was about to be completed, and we were supposed to move in from the lodgings we had been living in at the time of our detention. But I did not lose heart. Perhaps I regarded this act as a normal reaction of the counter-revolution. Perhaps I judged that we were just passing an important stage on the very long road which must lead us to final victory. Perhaps the still benign conditions of our imprisonment helped to reinforce this illusion.

The conditions in which I lived at *Bon Pasteur* were indeed far from dramatic. Being in prison means, and will always mean, being deprived of liberty. Prison is the most important manifestation of power in that it subjects everyone to its will. It is true that, in life, we are never completely free to do whatever we want. But a fair number of the activities we undertake, even when they are mandatory, such as school or work, are part of our identity, and can give us a sense of fulfilment, even bring pleasure. Life offers us a certain margin to choose our destiny. Prison is the opposite. When I was arrested I was deprived of what was most important to me: interacting with my peers in my social environment. While the others kept on walking, my feet were tied up. Still worse, it prevented me from studying. Instead of going to college, a breach formed in my mind, an enormous wound which for years afterwards would be difficult to heal.

But apart from that, the conditions of imprisonment at *Bon Pasteur* convent could not be compared with what would come later. And I cannot repeat often enough, I was not alone. The presence of people, both inside and outside the prison, was real and it took up an important space in my mind and my heart. It was a fundamental element that helped me to preserve my integrity and save my personality. But if this aspect seems positive to me today, that was not the case at the time.

IX

> Along the gallery under my windows and on the same level as my cell other prisoners, accompanied by under-warders and going to or coming from interrogation, used to pass from morning to night. [...] The sad sight increased my sufferings during the first few days, but little by little I became used to it until in the end it, too, lessened the horror of my solitude.
>
> Silvio Pellico, *My Prisons*[6]

In October 1975, after our case was provisionally closed, my husband was released, thanks to the fact, let me remind you, that the NEP had cancelled the decree by which it had put him at its disposal. Still nowadays, I wonder why the NEP did not release me, if the number of the decree that they applied to my husband was the same as they applied to me; but, whatever the reason, the fact was that while he was allowed to leave prison I was forced to stay in custody. His release caused a significant change in my own situation. A deep feeling of loneliness gradually invaded me. The members of his family, who had travelled each Sunday from Córdoba to visit us both, never came again. The meetings with him became less frequent. He had settled in Córdoba, where our families also lived. But despite the fact he could travel and had permission to visit me whenever he wished, paradoxically, he came less and less to see me. Furthermore, at *Bon Pasteur*, we did not have the intimacy we had enjoyed when I visited him every Thursday. Now, he insisted that we stay alone in the room reserved for visitors, while my sisters kept watch. But I refused. The nuns not only guarded me physically, but they had also besieged my mind. They no longer needed to check my movements, since now, I did that myself. My refusal brought about the first change in our relationship. He came to visit me sometimes accompanied by my eldest

---

6. Oxford University Press, 1963, p.20, translated by I G Capaldi from *Le Mie Prigioni. Memorie di Silvio Pellico, da Saluzzo*, 1832.

sister. During one of those visits, they stayed a very short time although the nuns would have given us the whole day had we wanted it. But they left. They had planned to spend the day somewhere in the mountains.

My husband explained to me that he needed rest and my sister added that she had to look after him. For security reasons, she could not leave him on his own. These explanations staggered me. Something disturbed me, but I did not know what. I probably did not want to recognise that it seemed a little bit strange that my sister wanted to look after my husband, now free, rather than come to support me in prison. From that day onwards, she did not come to see me anymore. As for him, he only came once or twice more.

From then onwards the conditions of my imprisonment were different. Time dragged. It was spring,[7] but I could not enjoy it. Moreover, the arrival of the warm weather only served to show me that I had just missed my year at college. I did not feel able to study any longer. Lessons had become too difficult to assimilate without the regular help of a teacher. By November, it had already become difficult for me to write letters, and when I did so I could not find much to say. This is what I then wrote to my family:

> Now the week is longer. Days become monotonous. I always try to do something, but I usually reach a moment at which boredom and deep melancholy are inevitable.
>
> All this is true. I have bad and quite sad moments. I miss you a lot and think of you intensely.
>
> It is odd. There is always a moment during the day (in general the evening), when I feel worn out. I have the impression I cannot cope, I do not know what to do.

Not having any reason to be taken to the men's prison, I could no longer enjoy those outings and beautiful much-awaited afternoons,

---

7. In the Southern hemisphere, spring starts in September.

during which I was surrounded by so many other political prisoners like myself, and their families. In *Bon Pasteur* convent, I was the only person detained for political reasons. The relationship with the ordinary prisoners was not always easy. For me, there were no differences between us. If I fought for a world without social classes, I could only consider the prostitutes women on an equal footing with me. For them, however, that was not the case. It was obvious that although I dreamt of a world without difference, in the world in which we lived differences in fact existed and were difficult to stand. Sometimes, aggressive prostitutes arrived in prison, and as soon as they saw me they decided that they did not like me. As a consequence, they treated me badly. With more experience of life and less naïve than I was, the nuns assigned me a separate room, exclusively for my use. Yet despite this, during the day I was exposed to the provocations of the other inmates and to their scorn. One day, I almost fell flat on my face because one of the prisoners tripped me up as I walked down the corridor.

Nevertheless, none of that seemed too serious to me. As I could share nothing with those inmates, I considered, as I wrote to my family, that the relationship was not "productive"; but for the rest, I observed what happened around me with a militant spirit and sociological curiosity. I thought that what I was experiencing was of the highest interest and contributed to my education. Furthermore, I gathered my courage not to allow myself to be engulfed by what at the time I called "bad moments". This is how I reassured my family:

> I am beginning to think more clearly, and I am rediscovering joy. I think a lot about you, about all my comrades and friends, and of course about my husband.
>
> I assure you that thinking about you, about thousands of past and present things, and also guessing a little bit about the future, floods me with a new hope, an indescribable happiness, something immeasurable.

But I had already noticed that the monotony and the routine were a danger. Despite my efforts to overcome the effect they had on my spirit, I started suffering from the distance from my loved ones. I no longer knitted with the enthusiasm I had at the beginning, but rather in a compulsive way to fill the empty moments and calm the boredom. I also found it hard to concentrate. Luisa was so fond of me that she soon realised days had become long and tedious for me. So, she decided to take me to the vegetable garden, on the opposite side of our section. Each time I was there, I looked at the street. Only a wall hardly higher than a hedge prevented me from being there. I only had to tell some friends to come and fetch me in a car, to leap over the hedge and to leave the country straightaway. But I knew the guard and the nuns trusted me and it kept me from doing anything other than noticing how easily I could have escaped. Consequently, I did not have any choice but to resign myself to my fate. The only alternative was to be transferred to the prison in the capital where there were other women political prisoners like me. I thought I would feel less isolated if I were with them; I would identify with them, I would share the time of my imprisonment and my activities with them.

I then asked my family and my lawyers to do everything possible to get me transferred to the prison at Córdoba. However, everything in the political environment in Argentina foretold of the seizure of power by the military, and when it was obvious that there would be a *coup d'état* I asked them to stop any move in that direction. If the Army took over, I would rather stay where I was, despite my "bad moments", under the control of the nuns. The level of perceptiveness I had at the time surprises me now. Although I was an activist in a political party, I cannot say I enjoyed particular lucidity in relation to national political affairs. I was also too young to have witnessed other acts of terror in the past.[8] In other words, I had never had the occasion to become aware of how the political game and corrupt management of institutions in Argentina gave rise to impunity. However, I clearly felt, not only that the *coup d'état* was imminent, but also the drama and terror it would trigger. This is why I

---

8. I had not read, for instance, the rigorous report by Rodolfo Walsh on the clandestine shooting of José León Suárez after the crushing of General Valle's insurrection in 1956, to re-establish the constitutional Government of Perón, deposed by the Army in 1955. This report, according to the author, dismissed any controversy about the veracity of the testimonies of the survivors: *Operación Masacre*, Buenos Aires, Planeta, Espejo de la Argentina, 1994 [1957].

sometimes wonder how so many Argentineans can, even today, say that they did not know what was happening in their country.

Solitary

X

> We don't live with History, or rather, we don't live
> History. We live our little life, the life of a group, of an
> instant of humankind, of an instant of world life.
>
> *Georges Simenon*

Although I no longer wished to be transferred to another prison, and despite my precautions, the police came to fetch me on December 13th 1975, to take me to the prison at Córdoba. I had to spend a night at police headquarters again, in a tiny cell, twice as small as the one, already reduced, in which I had been locked up immediately after my arrest. I slept in a niche of cement, somehow wrapped in a thin blanket. Despite the disagreeable conditions, the idea of travelling to Córdoba the day afterwards, where I would finally meet the political prisoners, alleviated my discomfort. Moreover, I knew how to make myself comfortable in any nook. Throughout our childhood, my mother, in response to any complaint made by my siblings or myself, reminded us that Swiss soldiers used to sleep on stones. This story, told by my grandfather about his nights spent at the frontier of his native country when he was a soldier during the First World War, bothered me. Still an adolescent, that night I wondered if my mother actually would have liked to see me sleep on stones. But it is also true that I had heard her discourse so often that it had finally succeeded in diminishing my wish for comfort and enhancing my ability to adapt to any situation.

The following day, after a two hour journey in a police van, we arrived in Córdoba. I was first taken to the Federal Police Headquarters for administrative procedures, and then to the Penitentiary Unity No. 1 of the San Martín area, where I was put in Hall 14. To reach it, I had to walk first along several corridors through the men's halls, and then, the alley between the cell blocks and the prison walls. The many iron doors I had to pass through, the ordinary prisoners crammed against the bars looking at me with their prurient expressions, and the mountains of garbage accumulated along the way, made me realise the difference between this prison and *Bon Pasteur* where I had come from. I particularly thought about my mother who, when she came to visit me, would have to go through all these places. But the desire to meet my new co-prisoners was stronger than any fear.

Hall 14 consisted of three floors. Unlike the old, dark, squalid buildings I had just seen, this one was new and clean. It had been built a short time earlier, according to high security standards. Originally, it was intended to hold ordinary prisoners considered dangerous but, ultimately, it was used to contain female political prisoners. Traditionally, women in Córdoba had also been imprisoned in *Bon Pasteur* convent, which, like that in Río Cuarto, served as a prison. But in May 1975 there had been a spectacular escape. A truck was used to pull out the bars of a window overlooking the street, hidden from the nuns' watchful eye by a blanket. This blanket was used as the backdrop of an improvised stage where the prisoners were performing a play while other inmates, who were supposed to be acting in the play, and who, by doing so, justified their presence backstage, jumped into the truck stationed in the street and made off without a sound. This convent-cum-prison no longer offered sufficient guarantees in the eyes of people in power, anxious to prevent any action by guerrillas to free their imprisoned comrades.

In Hall 14 of the penitentiary, each wing could accommodate forty women in individual cells. When I arrived, the cells on the ground floor were already full. On the first floor, there were still some empty cells. The second floor instead, was still completely empty. The majority of the women belonged to one or other of the two major extreme-left organizations, *Montoneros* and the People's Revolutionary Army (*Ejército Revolucionario del Pueblo*, ERP), whose struggle was based on guerrilla action. On the ground floor, there were only activists of the ERP. On the first floor, most of the prisoners belonged to *Montoneros*. There were also four prisoners who came from other minor political factions[9] and who had gathered into and independent group which they called the

---

9. *Frente Argentino de Liberación* (FAL), *Peronismo de Base, Partido Comunista* and an Anarchist organization.

Fringe. I was the only militant who belonged to *Vanguardia Comunista*, and therefore they included me in their group.

In general, the gap between the ideas we have of a situation and the reality is great, especially when we are young. The idea I had about life among political prisoners fitted my own needs and sensibilities at the time but had no relationship with reality. I was obviously frustrated.

Before I was finally settled on the first floor, the guard took me to the ground floor. I was welcomed with the warmth by which political prisoners usually greeted any newcomer who arrived in prison, as I had so many opportunities to observe afterward. They did indeed show a great spirit of solidarity. But later, I found myself with a small group in a cell, probably the one which had been assigned to me. I do not remember too many details of that moment, but I clearly keep in mind the image of one of the inmates. I learnt afterwards that she was one of the political leaders in the wing. I told of my experience with spontaneity and simplicity: where I came from, who I was, which political party I was an activist in, how and why I had been arrested. If the comrades from the Fringe, the group of independent political prisoners I met later, had not told me, I would never have realised that those prisoners from the ERP were actually interrogating me.

Soon afterwards, the guard told me that I would be transferred to the first floor. The prison authorities must have known perfectly well the political leanings of each prisoner, and in case they lacked data, the organizational structure within the prison itself provided them with it. Since it was known that only militants from the People's Revolutionary Army were on the ground floor, they must have realised that they had to take me to the other floor, where some inmates belonged to different groups. Just before my departure, the political leader who had participated in the supposed welcome meeting, handed me a pair of trousers that I had to deliver to another inmate on the first floor. I was glad I could be useful and do a favour. I did not know then that the prisoners were in the habit of using clothes as a means of communication. In this case, according to what my mates from the Fringe told me later, in the hem of the trousers I was carrying a written report on what I had said about myself.

At the end of the week, when I received the first visit from my mother and sisters, who at the time could still come into the hall and share an afternoon with me, I was able to observe an attitude of the same kind: one of the leaders of the People's Revolutionary Army pretended to be knitting next to us, although she was actually listening and checking what we were saying, and whenever we moved, she moved too.

I might be told that these stories are of no interest, that they are elements of no importance, or that they have no repercussion beyond the restricted sphere within which they happened. I might also be told that under the political circumstances we were living through, the revolutionary forces had to pay attention not to be infiltrated by the enemy. However, after I witnessed these apparently banal events, I became aware that prison was not as I had imagined. The political prisoners were divided according to their political beliefs. It meant that we were not all equal. What now seems obvious never occurred to me at the time. These elements, particularly the fact that I had been used to doing something without asking for agreement, generated despondency and disappointment.

Did my new co-prisoners' behaviour disappoint me because it smashed the idyllic image I had until then of political prisoners? Did it break the image of all of us in a uniform homogenous group, in prison for a common cause? Did the division in groups disappoint me because it excluded me from the majority? Did it disappoint me because, apart from the exclusion, I felt used and, consequently, humiliated? Did it disappoint me because I felt an object in relation to somebody to whom I had spoken with sympathy and friendship? Whatever it was, the first days in this new prison refuted my ideal conception of relationships based on implicit affinities, on generosity and spontaneity.

I was also troubled when I noticed that a prisoner remained in her cell when it was time to go to the courtyard. When I expressed my surprise to my neighbour, I was told she had been punished by her own comrades from the People's Revolutionary Army because she had given information to the police when she was arrested and tortured. At the time I was impressed. The fact that a person arrested by rightist reactionary agents had in turn to stay shut up by order of leftist militants disturbed me. At the time, I did not know how to integrate the idea. It was beyond my comprehension.

When I was at *Bon Pasteur* in Río Cuarto, I wished to be with the political prisoners in Córdoba. But now I could only add up the attitudes which made me feel uneasy and uncomfortable. On a certain day in summer 1976, the militants from *Montoneros* learnt that one of their political leaders, held in our same prison, had managed to escape. This escape, like that from *Bon Pasteur*, had also been spectacular. The prisoner had been transferred from the penitentiary to the court, where his lawyer was waiting for him. The latter had just opened his suitcase, taken out two guns, given one to his client, and together, following a violent shootout with police officers, they had run away. The joy shown by their companions in our wing drew my attention of course, but what shocked me most were the insults thrown at the guards, which seemed coarse and out of place. It was as if our projects for a new society were reduced to a vendetta, a fight between two gangs.

When I woke up the first morning in this new prison, I wanted to show myself enthusiastic and communicative. Coming out of the lavatories, jostled by the movement of all these women getting ready to start their day, I said hello to one of them with a smile, but she did not answer. When wishing to be transferred to Córdoba Prison, I had certainly expected to meet representatives of "the new man", people similar to this model of ideal man forged by Che Guevara, that we, activists for a better society, had talked so much about. In reality, I only met ordinary women, drowsy as they woke-up, tired and in a bad mood, anxious to respect the discipline imposed by their organizations.

Shortly after my arrival in this prison, when I wanted to leave my cell, a sharp pain in my gut stopped me. I remained bent double, unable to move. Just as a plant withers in an inhospitable environment, so my body reacted to the effects of a situation that was hard to bear. It acted as a barometer, beyond my control and resisting all my efforts to adapt to my new reality. The atmosphere in this new prison was hostile; I did not fit in it, and there was nobody to protect me and to support my right to be myself.

However, neither discomfort nor bad feelings prevented me from integrating into the community. After digesting my initial disappointments, I easily picked up the new habits shared by all prisoners. I would not deny that life in the blocks evolved in a positive manner, and that we even experienced joy. Despite being separated from society, we could still act in a concerted way. The most elementary form of human activity, which is, according to Hannah Arendt,[10] our ability to contribute something to the common world had not yet been destroyed. We could still develop certain activities, at the same time keeping an important margin of autonomy. But in general, my experience in prison made me think about power in a different way to what I did before being its victim. I was indeed surprised that once inside the wing, power did not remain on the threshold.

Outside of the prison, the repressive forces acted as we could have foreseen. We were worried, but the intensity of their actions was nothing compared to what would happen later. Because from a very young age I had positioned myself in opposition to any dominant power, these events did nothing to dampen my determination. In fact, they reinforced it. But, on the other hand, in prison I observed situations and attitudes which I would never have imagined before. Notwithstanding, a feeling of guilt made it impossible for me to speak about it for many years. Considering the horrors perpetrated later by the military authorities, I thought it inappropriate to speak on the manifestation of power within the prison block. Moreover, much later, every time I attempted to broach the subject with, for example, ex-political prisoners, intelligent and constructive dialogue, leaving aside any prejudice, was refused. It was as if, in the face of great historical events, small everyday gestures did not count. As if they had their meaning only in a restricted sphere of feelings and subjectivity and were insignificant compared to the transcendent nature of a more global reality. Still, those gestures have an influence on our personality and consequently on our way of participating in this reality and recreating it.

---

10. Hannah Arendt, *op. cit.*, p.475.

These acts, indeed, left deep traces in me, and at the time were among the factors that contributed, in spite of my having survived, to losing so much of my vitality and confidence to act. I was surprised by the similarities between my experiences and the story of Graciela Lo Prete about her time in Devoto Prison a year before the military coup. Despite the different circumstances, when I read her *Memoirs of a Political Prisoner*,[11] I felt spiritually at one with her. What she writes is similar to what I witnessed, first in Córdoba, then in the same prison at Devoto. That was what for years I described to the few friends I could confide in, without fearing their opinions, like a prison within a prison. I felt anxious when I said that what the military had done caused me much suffering, but no conflict or ambiguity; but within the prison, instead, everything was strange and complex, difficult to grasp.

Graciela says she had an idea that haunted her, and that when she met to talk with the prisoners from other left-wing organizations, those who did not belong to the two majority organizations within the prison, she always "revolved around the same thing":

> It's just so weird…When I was isolated in the cell at the federal police general quarters, I felt very lonely. I sang alone to hear a human voice, and also later in the cell of the court, in that small dirty square, while I waited to be called to testify, I felt a maddening loneliness. And right here, damn, are we not alone? They locked us and isolated us from the world. But them, you know? I've known them for a long time, I knew who they were and what to expect from them, imprisonment and violence were possible and I'd had my little armour ready for many years.
>
> But now this is not them anymore, we're splitting among ourselves.
>
> This is what's tremendous. We fight amongst ourselves and I feel that we are isolating ourselves…The wing is divided, there are many heavy silences, much bitterness in the throat, and why? We are fighting for very diffuse, very slippery issues…It's like a match about how *the new man* will be, and

---

11. *Memorias de Una Presa Política, 1975–1979*, Buenos Aires, Grupo Editorial Norma, 2006.

Solitary

when I look at ourselves in that match, I tell you, if it's going to be like this, I don't like it and I don't know who is going to want to become that man.

Given this conflicted situation within the wing, Graciela felt truly lonely, not lonely as when she was in the miserable cell of the federal police headquarters or in the court, but profoundly alone, with the loneliness one feels even when being surrounded by others, in that situation described by Arendt, in which one, without being isolated, feels totally abandoned. Graciela was hurt not only by the repression practised by the military, the police and the right-wing groups, but also by the repression which, confusingly, she felt among the inmates inside the prison:

> The thing is that, either because of what we discuss or for what we do not say, we are hurting ourselves. And there, indeed, I have no weapons, then, yes, I feel alone. If my friends isolate me…, then, yes, I feel lonely, I feel, how would I say? Another repression; what I say may sound outrageous, because you cannot compare, but I feel a repression that comes from another side and that hurts me more. It is very confusing all that I'm saying, isn't it?[12]

My feelings have also been confused for years, mixed with guilt and the impression that this was something I must not say. I felt deeply lonely, I had nobody to share my way of thinking with. After I finally managed to write about my experience, Graciela's story had a great impact on me. Talking to someone or opening a book may be enough for the feeling of loneliness to stop tormenting us.

---

12. Graciela Lo Prete, *op. cit.*, p.133, translated by the author.

XI

> Although I am a typical loner in daily life, my consciousness of belonging to the invisible community of those who strive for truth, beauty, and justice has preserved me from feeling isolated.
> Albert Einstein, *My Credo*[13]

Since my arrival on the first floor of Hall 14, I shared all my activities with the four jailmates from the Fringe. Other women belonging to minor left-wing political parties and groups arrived later and were also integrated with us. After the *coup d'état*, we were nine in all, united in this Fringe. Most of us had asked the guard to allocate us to cells at the end of the corridor. I was in cell No. 56. It was quite important to be next to these other companions. This allowed me to have a reference point and also friends. But life among us was not always easy. I found it particularly difficult to adapt to the discipline imposed by these women. In the prison of *Bon Pasteur*, the cell opening and closing times in the morning and the evening were imposed, but throughout the day I had the choice of organizing my itinerary as I wished. Nevertheless, I had not let myself fall into laziness and carelessness. On the contrary, I was always active and creative. I devoted certain moments to studying, reading and writing; at other moments, to sport, sewing and embroidery as well as to cooking and playing music. Instead, in the Córdoba Prison, from morning to evening I had to adapt to the programme of the group. The collective regime seemed so suffocating that, in the end, I did not even benefit from the moments reserved for myself.

Moreover, this discipline did not always correspond to what was expected of a person of my age at the time. It was no doubt stricter and more oppressive than that I would have expected at college or at home. My comrades imposed moments of study that were particularly boring

---

13. *Mein Glaubesbekenntnis*, written for the German League for Human Rights, Berlin/Caputh, 1932, translated by the author.

for me. I understood practically nothing of the subjects we discussed. Sometimes I interrupted the person who was reading to ask questions, but then I was reprimanded. These comrades had also decided that we would go out into the yard only in the mornings, and that in the afternoons we would study without interruption. I needed to be in the open air regularly, as I had been at *Bon Pasteur*, in what looked like the courtyard of a boarding school. The sky I saw from there was with me the whole day. Instead, here, in my new prison, I had the right to be outside for only two hours, on stony ground, and my older jailmates had decided to refuse one of these periods. In their eyes, the intensive study of dialectical materialism justified such an arbitrary decision.

Far be it from me to deny the importance of such a theoretical instrument in understanding how the world works, but at that moment I would have preferred to stop studying and enjoy the sun. This is why, by prohibiting every activity in the hall, the *coup d'état*, paradoxically, offered me a moment of relief. If I had known the consequences brought about by the presence of the military in the prison there is no doubt that I would have preferred to make a sacrifice and devote myself to reading *Anti-Dühring* by Engels, or at least to continue uncomprehendingly and be bored while others read. But the vision I had had at *Bon Pasteur* of the imminence of the *coup d'état* did not translate into images of clear and precise events — emotions and reason do not always correspond.

But beyond my boredom during the long hours devoted to studying, I felt uncomfortable in general. I had indeed wanted to change the social order, but my parameters and reference points still came from the world in which I had lived. Therefore, the other prisoners, probably considering themselves more revolutionary than me, questioned my attitudes and background. It was as if *being* had implied a predetermined form in itself. Without regard for my individuality or the complexity of my past life, they judged me according to the stereotype with which society is categorised into classes. I remember one story in particular, when I showed photos from my childhood. They had been taken during a Christmas party at my grandparents' house. I was surrounded by my family. Some time later, I spoke of my father's financial difficulties. After the failure of his business, he had abandoned us, leaving us in a state of abject misery, both materially and emotionally. Poverty and misery beat us cruelly. I was nine. I knew what hunger and cold meant, I felt my mother's anguish when we were ejected from our home and we had nowhere to go. Subsequently, I suffered from the absence of my father and the tears of my mother, who was unable to educate her children as she would have wished according to her cultural and social background. Despite the sadness I felt when I remembered this, my own story, when I shared it with my friends this led them to respond in a mocking tone that betrayed disbelief. They reminded me of the pictures I had shown them earlier, portraying a bourgeois lifestyle which precluded any possibility of having feelings. It was as if the obvious fact that I belonged to and came from a *petit bourgeoise* background excluded all possibility of my having feelings at all. I was moved when shortly after the *coup d'état*, one night, while we waited for the guard to lock each of us up in our individual cells, the woman from the last cell in the corridor looked at me with an expression of tenderness and admiration and said that I was pretty. If vanity there was, it was not as important as the surprise I had that someone could still have a pleasant image of me.

At school, two years earlier, two classmates had given me a pacifier. They believed that this symbol of childhood would compensate for my early maturity which manifested itself in my concern for social issues and the world in general. They had dared to categorise each of their classmates and had labelled them with the feature that, so they thought, best defined their personality. Now, in contrast, my cellmates in jail accused me of childishness. Perhaps this image allowed them to justify the way in which they addressed me. Paradoxically, their confidence to speak, their way of judging, and their habit of speaking beyond all doubt, infantilised me, and was detrimental to my mental and emotional autonomy. Their often authoritarian attitude did nothing but destroy any seeds of growth and intellectual independence. However, the structure within which we functioned offered me protection. These companions, as well as my belonging to the Fringe, were my points of reference within the prison, and there was no doubt that their authority was hugely important to me. I needed them to support my behaviour, and to confirm what was right or wrong. Moreover, some of them were true friends.

Solitary

My cell in Córdoba where we spent almost nine months of isolation, with the door shut most of the day. The picture was taken forty years later. The building is quite dilapidated, but the size is still the same.

XII

> [...] physical pain, the mutilation or diminution of the body gives solitude an absolute quality; it severs the slender bonds that even in the soul's deepest despair we are able to maintain between ourselves and others...
> Leonardo Sciascia, *The Council of Egypt*[14]

When I arrived at Córdoba Prison in December 1975, the same rules were applied to political prisoners as to ordinary prisoners. Thanks to this we "went to the movies" inside the prison once a week. There we met the male political prisoners from Halls 6, 8 and 9. We were also granted the right to a private visit. It was an intimate moment with our partners, whether they lived outside or were detained in the same prison. Some couples who had formed during the cinema sessions could also enjoy those moments which, compared to what came later, was a real privilege. My husband came from outside and we were together from six in the evening until nine o'clock the next day. But our relationship had changed, and I did not understand why. He kept repeating that I was hiding something. At the time, his insistence became a torment to me. I exhausted myself wondering if I really hid something without actually realising it.

At the movies I met a comrade of the party. He and I were the only militants of *Vanguardia Comunista* in Córdoba Prison. No doubt I enjoyed meeting him, but I never saw in him anything more than a comrade, a friend. However, my husband insisted so much about my hiding something, that I came to wonder if this fellow did not cause certain feelings in me that I did not dare confess. Perhaps, without knowing it, quite subconsciously, I was attracted to him.

In any case, the movie outings came to an abrupt halt. It was one of the first restrictive measures to be taken. The political situation was very

---
14. New York, Alfred A Knopf, 1966, p.183, translated by Adrienne Foulke from *Il Consiglio d'Egitto*, 1963.

tense, awaiting the arrival of the military to power. Private visits instead, were still kept up for some time. But my relationship with my husband was becoming painful; above all it was losing its freshness and spontaneity. During one of those visits he finally told me that, when he had been released from prison, he had slept with my sister. Then I understood why they had left so hastily when they had come to visit me at *Bon Pasteur*, and the subsequent change in his attitude. I did not speak again for the whole night, and the next day, still without talking, I returned to my wing. Seen from my current perspective, this experience may even seem banal. Extra-marital sexual relations are undoubtedly as old as the institution of marriage itself. It is an aspect that comes with it, hidden by social hypocrisy. But back then this did not appear so clearly to me and it was traumatic and painful having to live through it.

At that moment I could not put a name to what I felt. But despite my confusion, I realised that, for months, my husband had tried to transfer responsibility for something he had done, and did not know how to own, onto me. The following week he was granted a special visit on my birthday. That day I was eighteen. Neither of us had much to say. Before the visit was officially over, I asked the guard to take me back to the wing. The following Saturday was a day of men's visits and my husband could visit me inside our wing. But beside him my father had also come to visit me. It turned out to be a sad afternoon.

To my husband nothing seemed more important than talking about what had happened. But I had to welcome my father. So, I told my husband everything was fine, which was somehow true. By telling me what had really happened, he lifted the psychological pressure he had exerted over me by accusing me of keeping a secret. After all, his relationship with my sister seemed less serious than the process he had dragged me through following it. They had, in fact, had a brief relationship before our own began. Their encounter, in the conditions of isolation and instability which he had probably felt on leaving prison, was not entirely surprising.

But now he seemed to feel a storm inside him, and flatly refused to understand that there really might be something else apart from what bothered him. During his visit, he appeared tormented and refused to see reason. He did not allow me to stay with my father and took me to my cell to speak with me. But we were interrupted by another inmate who asked me to go and fetch my father because he was disturbing her privacy with her own father. My husband had no choice but to wait, as a result of which, when the visit reached its end, he did not want to leave. A deep helplessness invaded me. The man I had in front of me was my husband and he would not understand that we were in prison, that I had to stay inside, and he had to go. The guard hardened her tone as she repeated her call, until finally he left. It was the last time I would see him before arriving in exile in France two years later. This visit would indeed be the last one we would have before the military coup, some days later.

These events certainly had an impact on me, and my body so testified. I had always desperately wanted to have children and while at *Bon Pasteur* I had thought about having a baby. I used to say that if I had to stay there much longer I would have one. But when the threat of a *coup d'état* was imminent and the change in the political climate no longer made it suitable to generate life, I stopped thinking about moving to Córdoba and stopped dreaming of a baby. After moving into the new prison, shortly after my husband finally told me what was poisoning our relationship, I began to suffer from amenorrhoea, which lasted for seven years. At that moment, however, I found the practical aspect more important than the physiological and psychological complications, of which I would only become aware later. Given the circumstances to which the military subjected us, when we lacked even a piece of cotton, I thought my body was doing me a favour by interrupting my menstrual cycle.

More serious complications were caused by vaginal inflammation. When I went to see the prison's hospital doctor, I had to explain what was affecting me in front of other detainees who were there for other disorders. Among them was one of my friends from the Fringe. When I talked to the doctor, I explained in detail what my symptoms were, as graphically as possible. The doctor prescribed an anti-inflammatory medication which had to be applied locally with a syringe and a douche. Back on the wing, I went to my cell. I sat reading quietly on my bed, my torso leaning against the wall protected by the pillow, and with my legs comfortably extended. Occasionally, I ate almonds which I drew from a small bag my mother had brought me. She had recommended I eat several a day to give me strength. Suddenly, I heard one of the inmates who had been with me in the hospital. She was in the cell opposite to mine, talking with another inmate from the Fringe. She was laughing so much that she had trouble speaking. She repeated what I had explained to the doctor and, above all, she put emphasis on the type of description I had given him. At that moment, something in me stopped working. I felt my body paralysed, I felt heat and a strong pressure on my temples; mentally, I remained speechless. I started eating one almond after another and within seconds had devoured the entire packet.

That woman was the person I admired and respected most among us. I found her intelligent and tried to follow her example. But now she was mocking me. Today I understand that these are things that unfortunately happen when one is deprived of the intimacy, privacy and confidentiality that is essential during a visit to a doctor; I also understand that I had the misfortune for her to be near the scene of the story and listening-in. Who has not made fun of someone else once in their life, without it involving any particular feeling against them, or mockery or hostility. But at the time I could think none of this. I was young and felt particularly bad about it.

A few days later, when the military arrived at the jail, they forced us to go out into the yard, put us against the wall and ordered us to undress. While some of them watched us pointing their guns with an outrageous look, others turned our cells upside down and looted them. When we went back inside, among the few individual items they had left behind the syringe and vaginal douche lay visibly in the corridor, as if they wanted to symbolise the humiliation of women, both collectively and individually.

XIII

That was the way we spent the evening hours when the door of our cell might open at any moment and the death order sound for one of us [...]

We lived through that time of horror. We think of it now with surprise at our own feelings. How strangely people are built—we can bear the unbearable.

It is impossible, however, to prevent such times from leaving deep traces on our lives. They lie in little rolls of film under the membrane of our brain, and unroll in the form of insanity some time later in real life—if we ever live that long. Or perhaps they will unfold later in the form of great cemeteries, or green gardens planted with the most precious seed of human lives.

Julius Fucik, *Notes From the Gallows*[15]

We do not speak. Each one tries to be ready. Each one is afraid for himself [...] Ready to die, I think we are; ready to be pointed out at random to die, not.

Robert Antelme, *The Human Race*[16]

The military arrived at the Penitentiary Unit of the City of Córdoba in the wake of the *coup d'état* of March 24th 1976, led by General Jorge Rafael Videla.[17] They acted on the orders of General Luciano Benjamín Menéndez,[18] commander of the Third Army Corps, and General Juan Bautista Sasiaiñ, commander of the Fourth

---

15. *Op. cit.*, p.76.
16. *Op. cit.*, p.142.
17. Videla was later sentenced to life imprisonment and died in prison in May 2013, aged 87.
18. Menéndez died in prison in February 2018, aged 90, having been given 13 life sentences for crimes against humanity.

Airborne Brigade. We were then completely cut off. Young mothers were separated from their babies. For nearly nine months we were prevented from seeing our families and friends and were deprived of all contact with the outside world. They came to our cell blocks on April 2nd. We were stripped of everything, of the basic necessities of daily life as well as objects of sentimental value, such as letters or pictures. They left us with just our clothes and blankets. When we returned to our cells after the first sacking, the wing resembled a village plundered by the Huns. It revealed in miniature the shame and the abuse with which the military government and its economic policy, enforced by the Minister José Martínez de Hoz, would dismantle the country.

A few days after the arrival of the military, the prison authorities came to fetch me to make me sign the final ruling of the Court of Appeals. The judgement confirmed that none of my actions had violated the law established by the national institutions and said that my case was, therefore, definitively closed. But if earlier, when my case was temporarily closed, the NEP had decided to keep me in prison, arguing that I constituted a risk to national security, now that the Army had formally established its control over the whole State, my release was even less likely. The military did not recognise any law other than their own, and they decided the fate of people as they wished.

They came several times a day to our wing. They arrived without warning and with brutality. Each time they came, we had to stand in front of our cells, with our backs towards the corridor, heads bowed and hands behind us. Whatever we were doing when they arrived, even when we were in the shower, we had to rush to take up this position. At first, they came mainly to make us "dance". That was what they called the endless military-style gymnastics they forced us to do. On several occasions, they kept us awake throughout the night, forcing us to do exercises. If we did get the opportunity to lie down, we would just have settled to sleep when another group of soldiers would arrive with even crueller orders. And this continued in the same manner for hours on end. These gymnastics, although violent, were basic. Each prisoner, in front of her cell, had to bend her knees, get up, take a step towards the inside of the cell, another back and start again. We had to move more and more quickly, at the pace set by the shouts of the soldiers, for hours and hours without stopping. The day after the first workout, our muscles seized up; some inmates could not walk without the help of other prisoners. Pregnant women had received permission not to exercise. Instead, soldiers forced them to make circles with their arms outstretched and to blink their eyes, for hours on end. Controlling those movements seemed to be very important for the soldiers of the national army. On the other hand, when a woman stopped and said she could not continue because she had her period, they were embarrassed. They did not know how to react, having probably never before heard anybody speak about menstruation.

On one occasion, they forced us to do gymnastics in a particularly cruel way that could have had serious consequences. That day, the soldiers were furious, a sign that they had been dealt a devastating blow by the guerrillas. They made us alternate between push-ups and walking, moving towards the front of the wing. Three push-ups, stand up, take a step, repeat three push-ups, and so on. Upon reaching the gates, they made us turn left to the bathroom. Now, not only was the space more confined, but at some point we could not move any further. The force with which the military's orders echoed, however, precluded any possibility of stopping. The prisoners who were at the front were on the verge of suffocation and believed they would die.

Despite the brutality and the baseness to which the military subjected us, the impact they caused when they first broke into the wing, and the fear we felt, each time they left we gathered in small groups in the middle of the corridor to comment on what had taken place, and we laughed as much as we could. Many of their attitudes seemed clownish to us. Their tough, macho bravado failed to hide their upset and embarrassment when confronted by forty young women. The ridiculousness of their behaviour was a source of amusement to us.

We once laughed at a threat made by an officer. He was a captain pacing the corridor, shouting moralistic remarks in military-style. All privileges were suspended. The ladies' college was over! Now we would see what real discipline was. Among other measures which threatened more difficult times, he warned us that we would be served salty pea soup and would then be deprived of water. A few days later, we did indeed eat very salty pea soup. None of us remembered the earlier threat. We were reminded only when we found out that there was no water in the taps. We were dying of thirst and returned to our cells where we would be held locked-up until the following day with our throats on fire. In spite of the discomfort we endured, we often joked about this episode.

Even the day they cut our hair, the laughter provoked by how we looked prevailed over the fatigue caused by the wait and the anxiety of this humiliation. That day, soldiers arrived in the morning. We were locked in our cells. We had no idea what was happening. The hours passed and the silence kept us from knowing what they were scheming, or even if they were still in the wing. At noon, we heard the sound of the carriage bringing the meals, but we were not summoned to eat or drink or go to the bathroom. When one of the soldiers came to our cells, we realised that they were cutting prisoners' hair. We had to show the utmost docility. Was it a metaphor for female genital mutilation—which does not exist in our cultural practices—the cutting of another of our feminine attributes?

Late in the afternoon, they left us and we could finally go out into the corridor. Our appearance was certainly miserable, but we did not cry. Quite the contrary, the authenticity of our laughter was proportionate to how they had damaged us and made us look ridiculous. They had cut my hair to my neck in three different lengths. A few days later, thankfully, the guard passed us a pair of scissors that allowed us to improve our looks. My new haircut led some of my friends to call me *The Little Prince*. This helped me not to miss my long hair too much.

But the laughter died away. The gymnastics and the intention to impose military discipline on political prisoners gave way to repressive measures of extremely brutal violence, to punishments, transfers and even assassinations. Is it possible to imagine what it is like to say goodnight to other women without knowing who would or who would not be there the next morning? Can anyone understand the feeling of lying alone in a cell, listening out for sounds of a padlock being undone and chains being slid, for the sound of boots walking without knowing at which cell they might stop? And finally, how is it possible to imagine, from the outside, what you feel when you hear those same boots when they leave in the silence of the night and a comrade is taken to be executed some time later? Why her and not me? To this question, we say that such an outcome will never be ours. This calms us and allows us to continue to survive.

The most dramatically "silent" day of 1976, and maybe also the coldest, was the 14th of July, when only the shouts of fellow prisoners being tortured broke the silence. I do not remember all that well the details of these events. With time, images fade and dissolve in a sea of different sensations among which it is difficult for me to distinguish what caused them. But, at the same time, every time an external event rekindles these experiences in me, I have the impression in my heart of hearts that to believe that one can forget is just an illusion. One can only have periods of respite where one feels reassured and can believe that one can live, and have aspirations and ambitions like anybody else.

I know that I was there and I believe I know how things happened, but my memories are concentrated around some images which, in my spirit, represent all that I lived and felt at that moment. I remember that two women coming from the cells on the second floor, which at the time were intended for solitary confinement, were led to a yard which adjoined our building. One of them was pinned half naked to the ground and released only after she had shouted the Argentinean Army's praises and predicted death for the People's Revolutionary Army, to which she belonged. I remember that soon afterwards, she and the other prisoner had to cover over graffiti painted on the walls of the yard, vestiges no doubt of our activities during our time in the yard in the summer before the military coup. While one of them used a paintbrush, the other was forced to do it with her hand. At two o'clock in the afternoon, another prisoner, José René Moukarzel, was brought to the yard. At the time, I did not know anything about him; it was said that he was a doctor, and everybody called him The Turk, which in Argentina indicates nationals of Arabic origin; something of a generalisation. I thought he was forty-years-old, but he was actually only twenty-six. He had not wanted to give the name of an ordinary prisoner who helped the political prisoners to send information outside the prison. He had been hit when being interrogated before being brought to the yard where he was tied up, half naked, feet and hands fastened to four pickets nailed down to the ground. The soldier who watched him regularly poured buckets of cold water on him. After a while, stones were placed under his back, level with his kidneys. For hours, José's howls rose from the yard, like those of a lamb being slaughtered. For hours, his shouts of agony resounded in the sepulchral silence of our wing. Late at night, he had a cardiac arrest and died.

Even if it remains relatively hazy in my mind, I remember that the woman who had not been pinned to the ground was forced to fill the bucket with fifty litres of cold water and to pour it over José, under the threat of being tied to the ground herself. Around me, other prisoners did not miss the opportunity to condemn the attitude of the two women in the yard, one for agreeing to shout slogans in favour of the junta, the other for torturing the man. At that moment, I did not dare to consider what I would have done in the same situation. My capacity to ask myself this question was pushed aside by a welling-up of confusion that increasingly undermined my mental wellbeing. My ideology and my political commitment did not allow me to oppose my companions. But my internal defences weakened so much that I did not succeed in uttering the slightest judgment.

I felt the same thing when the military asked me to get undressed. Previously, they had forced us to strip ourselves, all of us together; now, they imposed this humiliation in an individual way. They chose the youngest prisoners. With my companions from the Fringe we had decided to resist these assaults. One night, a non-commissioned officer, Corporal Pérez, came into my cell and asked me to take my nightdress off. As I refused to comply, he did it by force. I started shouting to alert the guard, which forced the non-commissioned officer to leave. An officer came in response to the commotion and forced me to undress completely. He then put his hand between my legs, spread them out by striking my thighs abruptly and inserting two fingers into my vagina. Faced with such a demonstration of power, I did not dare shout again. He left me to ruminate silently on this new humiliation. I do not know where I found the courage to face Corporal Pérez the first time, but in this case, the assurance and the authoritarian tone of the officer had blocked me from reacting against his will.

This officer returned a little later accompanied with his superior, the highest-ranking officer we had ever met. He declared that the Argentinean Army was there to take care of us and to protect us and he asked me to tell him what had happened. While he spoke, the man who had abused me looked at me fixedly with his emerald green eyes, with such a devilishly strong look that I did not dare accuse him. I limited myself to speaking about what had happened first and accusing Corporal Pérez. They promised to put him under arrest for a month. The idea that he would be locked-up alone in a cell for so long made me feel guilty. A feeling of cowardice and pettiness finally took my confusion to its height.

Corporal Pérez, who was a subordinate, poor and dark-skinned man, was going to be punished, but I had not done anything to prevent the other officer from giving himself the role of rescuer. The rest of what I felt, I could not perceive. The sensations of the body do not know friendship, philosophy or ideologies. So, they often escape our control. I had to condemn the gesture of the officer towards my intimacy and not pay attention to the forbidden sensations which could search for other ways to manifest themselves in me. That is why, once again, the presence of my companions and the dialogue with them allowed me to find a precise answer and to ignore the oppression which tightened my heart.

Solitary

XIV

> And I repeat, we live for happiness, for that we went to battle, for that we die. Let grief never be connected with our name.
> Julius Fucik, *Notes from the Gallows*[19]

> Loss of freedom in itself changes everyone to the roots of his being. If the daily torment of being a prisoner includes the unceasing fear of death, the shock inflicted on the prisoner is so profound that his reactions can no longer be called normal.
> Margarete Buber-Neumann, *Mistress to Kafka*[20]

Diana was the first prisoner the military came to pick up. That was on April 18th 1976; but they brought her back some days later. She had much less hair; they had torn it torturing her. However, Diana had neither lost her vitality nor her joy. But they came to fetch her again in the night of the 17th May, and that time it was forever. The next day, a prisoner who had been staying at the prison hospital in front of our hall informed us that that same night, they had killed her. While the windows of the cells on the right of the wing overlooked the outside wall of the prison and therefore prevented any further vision, those of the cells on the left gave onto the inside of the prison and, consequently, had to be completely sealed twenty-four hours a day so as to prevent any communication with the rest of the prisoners. But two of our inmates from the Fringe broke the rules and communicated with this prisoner in the hospital with extreme caution, using sign language. He had the right to read newspapers and then was able to supply them with details. Diana together with five other prisoners from the men's hall killed that same night were the first prisoners to whom the military

---
19. *Op. cit.*, p.51.
20. English version, Guildford and London, Billing & Sons Limited, 1966, pp.18–19.

applied the sinister practice of transfer and shooting on an isolated road, giving the excuse that they had tried to run away. The list of our companions murdered in this way increased in the months that followed: the military killed twenty-nine inmates from Córdoba Prison. Diana was 23.

Life inside the wing continued nevertheless. A short time later, members of Diana's organization asked the guard to open the door of her cell for them to recover the objects which had remained inside and which, they said, belonged to them. The guard accepted this. Some of them then rushed to take the clothes of the missing person. Before the military *coup d'état*, Diana received visits from her father and her fiancé, both from Buenos Aires. They brought her clothes that were apparently more expensive than those the families of the majority of prisoners could afford and that therefore provoked not only the admiration of the other prisoners but also their greed. I remember the long nightdress, red with white stripes. When Diana received it, it caused a sensation and raised a lot of chatter accompanied with naughty comments. Now, having learnt of Diana's death, several prisoners claimed it. Each one of them claimed that Diana — who had certainly thought of distributing her clothes to her companions because she also knew that the military would come to fetch her — had left them the nightdress as an inheritance. The scene of those prisoners inside the cell evoked visions of the cinema film *Zorba the Greek*, where villagers hurried up to Madam Hortense's door, the dying foreigner, to seize the garments the lady had brought along with her from elsewhere. But in our prison, we were not supposed to be dealing with old harpies, neighbours in a small village, but with political prisoners, with women who, in my eyes, had been militants for a higher set of values and for a better world. I saw the young woman who had managed to grab the nightdress leave the cell. Her face shone with joy and showed a smile of shameless triumph. As the other prisoners refused to believe that Diana had promised her the nightdress she declared that, in any case, the dead do not speak.

The military also took one of my Fringe companions, but they brought her back after a certain time. In the interim, she had been in a concentration camp. On her return to the prison, she informed us about the existence of "Boards of Recognition". These boards were comprised of members of the major leftist organizations who had agreed to collaborate with the repressive forces of the police or army. They were supposed to recognise the activists in the photos presented to them by the torturers and to supply all the information they had about them. They were also taken, day after day, in the infamous, terrifying dark-tinted cars used by the paramilitary bands. They then pointed out the places where other activists lived. Three women from *Montoneros* forced to do this work of denunciation, our companion said to us, looked like zombies. They gave the impression of being complete aliens, the only way, we thought many years later, to do something that otherwise would have never been acceptable.

Apparently, these three women must have denounced the person inside the prison responsible for their political organization. This person guaranteed contact with the outside world, that is, the flow of all information between the inside and the outside of the prison, this being the reason these collaborators knew her and had had contact with her before they themselves were arrested. As a result of this denunciation, the military came to search her cell and found a notebook. It was hidden inside the cell door which consisted of two parts: a wooden board, lined with a board made of metal. The two parts were not completely stuck to each other, leaving a crack. Furthermore, the doors were unfinished: the frame of the small window on the top of the door, which served to allow communication with the outside of the cell, had not yet been installed. It was possible to slide objects between the two boards. Those objects, instead of continuing their natural fall to the ground, remained stuck halfway, due to the projections of the badly finished wooden boards. Having been informed about the notebook by the collaborators in the concentration camp, the military came to our wing and went directly to the door of the leader's cell. There they inserted a long piece of wire and found the notebook with all the elements to prove that *Montoneros* were preparing an escape plan for its leaders. An element of fundamental importance to guarantee the success of this escape was the lorry which usually passed along the corridor below the hall loaded with sacks of pasta. In all likelihood, although I cannot figure out how they would succeed in tearing the window off the wall, the prisoners would let themselves fall on these bags and hide under them. This is all I remember of this story.

Two elements of these episodes had an important impact on me that I could not explain at the time. The fact that in a concentration camp there were prisoners who collaborated with the torturers is one to be found in any armed conflict and in any repressive and oppressive system in general. For me, however, it was new. Now I knew that it could happen to anyone, and that, consequently, I had to distrust even my neighbour. Along with my trust, my ingenuousness also disappeared, which did not mean, however, an increase in my lucidity. It only added to my perplexity regarding events.

The other element whose impact on me I did not know how to measure at the time was my discovery that, for some prisoners, every life did not have the same value. The escape plan they had conceived would no doubt have given the military an excuse to massacre those who had not taken part in it. Moreover, my presentiment was confirmed some years later by a defrocked priest from Córdoba, exiled in Paris. From this period onwards, there were frequent power cuts during the night. The first time we found ourselves in the twilight we were seized by a terrible foreboding. Our panic was almost tangible in the atmosphere of the wing. Familiar as we were with the light being switched on for the whole night, the sudden darkness seemed to deliver a coded message, an omen of horror. We must have been very acquainted with the idea of what could happen to us because as soon as the light was turned off nobody dared to speak. The atmosphere was lugubrious, the silence heavy. When one of the prisoners timidly tried to call the guard, we made her shut up with energetic shushing sounds, uttered spontaneously by all of us at the same time. A climate of expectation, of alert to any noise could be felt. A very distant sound, indefinable, was heard. Darkness made it more powerful. Only that was heard. It was a dull, metal noise. It was like a siren which sounded far away announcing our death. Given my mental state of the time, I had the impression that thousands of soldiers were walking towards us. The noise of boots seemed so clear, first steps, then a battalion, a sound so perceptible that it seemed real. They all came towards us, they came to kill us. After that, the silence was total.

Power cuts continued for a certain time. Generally, they took place during the night, but once they occurred while we were having dinner. According to what this priest friend of mine told me later, they were part of a plan masterminded by the military: they wanted to dig a tunnel so as to create the appearance of an escape plan by the political prisoners in the penitentiary, and thus find the excuse to kill us all. In fact, the Army could get rid of those they kidnapped and took straight to the concentration camps or clandestine detention centres with total impunity, but they could not do the same with those who were in prison. Most of us had been arrested before the military *coup d'état*, and therefore, we had a lawfully recognised status. If they wanted to exterminate us, they had to find a justification, and an attempt to escape was ideal. But according to this friend, this project was abandoned when it reached the ears of the Archbishop of Córdoba, Cardinal Primatesta. If such was the case, the church, for once, suspended its complicity with the national army.

In spite of the panic spread during the first power cut, not only did I remain calm, but I had no lack of heroic spirit. At some moments, I had the certainty that the military were coming to kill us. I had never felt death so near. I then concentrated on the images of my family and my husband. I felt that I was going to die, but by mentally projecting the image of myself that I was going to leave for them, I easily managed to assimilate the idea of death.

However, moments of boldness and bravery are short-lived and temporary, and the courage required to throw oneself into big exploits or to put one's life in danger may not be as difficult to find as is the one we need to face, daily, a situation in which we are condemned to total passivity. Furthermore, the eighteen years I had then lived were insufficient to allow me to comprehend all the elements I was experiencing and observing in this, our new reality, without causing collateral damage.

I had taken militant action in accordance with clear and precise values, without any ambiguity, and according to principles which kept us always alert, never overcome by fatigue or adversity, never bowed in front of the enemy. Influenced by Fucik's writings and avid to respect his last wishes, we felt the obligation to live for joy, to go into battle and be ready to die. But confronted by this experience in prison, it was difficult for me to comprehend a range of human feelings and behaviour which did not fit the narrow confines of resistance, virtue or exemplary nature.

Before my arrest, it had been clear to me that the police or the military could arrest us, torture us and even kill us, and I believed I shared the idea of the attitude that my companions and I should adopt. Now, instead, confronted by such complex circumstances and unable to share my impressions about what was happening with practically anybody, I did not know what to think any more. The impossibility of understanding our difficult and complicated situation according to my usual values gave way to a deserted world, devoid of elements which would have allowed me to find an answer to the new questions with which terrible reality bombarded us. Now, it was no longer a question of dying as a hero, but of knowing which ideas and values to recuperate when we managed to survive to resume a daily life.

XV

> But the interrogation wasn't the worst of it. The worst was coming back to the same room with the same table, the same bed, the same washbasin, the same wallpaper.
> Stefan Zweig, *Chess*[21]

> What flustered me was not so much the interrogations but the slowing of time. Hours turned to days, and days turned to weeks in the suffocating sameness of my cell. I prayed five times a day. I stretched and attempted calisthenics.
> Shirin Ebadi, *Iran Awakening*[22]

Submerged in uncertainty, however, confused by the new circumstances, what was most important at the time was that my companions were there. We were still forty prisoners in the wing. Some events, although very few, still occurred, and this helped to alleviate our degree of isolation. We had no contact with the outside, but we could communicate among ourselves. When, after their arrival at the prison, the military forced us to remain locked in our cells most of the time, we could still see companions in cells on the opposite side through the small window in the door. We heard the voices of other companions we could not see. During the hours when we were allowed to speak, we did so alternately, from each of our cells towards the whole wing. We took pleasure in telling anecdotes and recollections, or we exercised our memory by recounting novels, films, journeys and stories of any kind. Any narration was welcome to populate our hours of total inactivity.

It is true that, because of my young age, my repertoire was not vast, but also because at home we had neither radio nor television, I was

---
21. London, Penguin Books, 2006, p.39, translated by Anthea Bell from *Schachnovelle*, 1943.
22. With the collaboration of Azadeh Moaveni, New York, Ebury Publishing, 2006, p.171.

able nevertheless to tell the story of the movie *The Sound of Music*.[23] I focused on the love story between the main character, interpreted by Julie Andrews, and Captain von Trapp. This was the aspect of the film which had held my attention when I had seen it at the age of eleven. I also remembered with amusement the sequence of the seven children who had eaten blackberries and were betrayed by the colour of their tongues. The backdrop, which was the occupation of Austria by the Nazis, and the consequent flight of the Von Trapp family to Switzerland, had passed completely unnoticed by me. I realised this only when I saw the film again, some years later in Paris.

The other prisoners, for their part, described beautiful places which they had visited at home and abroad. They also spoke about desserts such as *dulce de leche* and *banana split*. As they said, the latter was the best dessert in Argentina. At home we did not eat *dulce de leche*. Although it is the most commonly eaten sweet in my country, it is a manufactured product, and has to be bought from a shop. Money being scarce at home, rather we ate fruit jams that my mother and I made together. I had not visited any of the tourist zones the women spoke about, I had never been to the most famous sites they described, and I had never seen the sea. During my holidays, I used to go to my grandparents in Esperanza, a city that nobody had heard of, although it was the first agricultural settlement in the country, the main reception centre for European immigrants. At that time, my companions' stories allowed me to imagine all the journeys I would make and all the good things I would eat when I was released.

Towards the end of the winter, harassment in our prison became rarer. The military stopped coming to the wing. After the horrors at the beginning, nothing more happened. We had to remain locked in our cells for much longer, and the hours spent in silence seemed to drag. To overcome a tendency to apathy and low spirits, not only did I walk, but I also counted my steps each time, backwards and forwards, in the cell. Having no goal to reach, or people, or objects, or any event to entertain me along my way, or even any possibility of modifying my path, this diverted me from the reality of desolation, and helped me keep mentally

---

23. Robert Wise, USA, 1965.

active. As I wrote to my sister when I finally had the occasion to do so some months later:

> Sometimes, I wanted to remain immobile all morning long. But I did all I could to keep my spirits up. Otherwise, I would have felt very bad. I had to resist the urge to throw everything over and let myself go. This is at least what happened to me. And you know, even though it seems to be a subject without any interest, such is not the case. It is very important, especially in such a situation as the one we had to go through in Córdoba.

To relieve the weight of this situation, to avoid being overcome by inactivity, I had set myself the goal of walking at least one thousand five hundred turns a day in both directions. Since the distance covered by every length was two metres, I finally walked three kilometres. When I reached my objective, I had nothing else to do but count. The opaque glass window of the cell had five squares along its length and five across its width, so twenty-five small squares in all. Nine squares in the middle of those twenty-five squares belonged to the small window, which, before the soldiers forbade it, opened as an attic window. Apart from the twenty-five small squares of the window in the centre, there were those of the sides: ten small squares; two rows of five squares each. There were forty-five small squares in all, easy to count. Two, four, six, eight, ten, I covered a side. Five, ten, eleven, twelve, thirteen, fourteen, fifteen and sixteen, I went along the nine panes which formed the small central window. Furthermore, every small square contained a large number of smaller squares, formed by the metal net inside the glass, like the material used when constructing high security buildings. I counted them as well. The numeric combinations were then infinite. To those, I could add the tiles of the floor; I just had to turn my head to the left, and look at the ground: two, four, six, eight, ten squares, and my eyes reached the door. I could also count the four steps of the ladder which led up to the bed, and the five tiles on the floor, counted in their horizontal sense. Sitting on the concrete slab below the window, I could count endlessly.

But when it was time to leave the cell, or when we were allowed to speak, I could *alternate*. Once again, the presence of my companions offered me fundamental support. I could also interrupt my counting to chat discretely with my neighbour in cell No. 57, during the hours when it was forbidden to speak. She belonged to the Fringe as well. Breaking the rules, I went up to my bed in the high part of the wall and I cautiously slid the glass of the lamp embedded in the opposite wall. Then I called my neighbour so that she did the same on her side. By this means, we could communicate. We each sat on our respective mattresses, which we had to fold in two when we woke up in the morning, and, she in her cell, I in mine, we could chat. It was almost as if we were visiting each other and having a nice cup of tea. We had to speak in a very low voice and be attentive to the possible arrival of the guard in the wing. One of them, particularly perverse, opened the padlocks and doors noiselessly so that she could catch us red-handed and reprimand us. But apart from that, it was a real pleasure to be able to share a moment with my neighbour. We especially remembered anecdotes of our free life. She was not much older than me. She often scolded me, but I loved her as a sister.

It also happened that a prisoner sometimes surprised us with her skills. Once, for instance, when the cells were opened and we could go out and meet in the corridor, one of them showed quite a small jumper to us; it was so tiny that it could hardly have wrapped a newborn guinea pig. The conditions and the tools with which she had done it gave the pullover a particular beauty and aroused an exceptional tenderness in us. During the hours of silence and solitude, she had opened the box of the lamp embedded in the wall and retrieved two nails forgotten by the workmen during the construction of the building. Then, she had taken a red sock, and had undone it. With the fibre that she recovered, using the nails as needles, she had knitted this mini-jumper.

Perhaps less creative, but certainly no less skilful, another prisoner appeared one day with a hairless arm. During her hours of idleness, she had managed to tear all the hairs off one of her arms with her fingertips. This did not take long to become fashionable and widespread throughout the wing. From the arms, it extended to the legs, and then to the armpits. It was not only a pastime, but also resolved the problem caused by lack of deodorant.

After a time, however, the moments of silence stretched out and our tendency to retreat into ourselves increased. The situation we were in, the revelation of the "Boards of Recognition" which exposed the existence of collaborators who provided information to the military, as well as the fact that the isolation seemed endless, certainly modified the way we related to each other. The collection of books, films, journeys and stories to be told progressively ran out. The exchange between my neighbour and me, so pleasant in the beginning, decreased as well. The recollections of our life before being arrested faded under the weight of the accumulation of empty days in prison. So, I stepped up my routine of counting. If, in the beginning, I had dreamed for hours about my future life outside, gradually, without really noticing it, my beautiful mental images were replaced by numbers. Even my craving for sweets was successfully replaced by my meticulous counting. But despite everything, although with diminished enthusiasm, we felt the presence of others again, and it saved us from total nothingness. It still allowed us to *alter* the reality. Nothingness then, was no more than a threat.

Solitary

XVI

> When the winter began, prisoners were allowed to receive
> parcels from outside [...] The first parcel was an event in
> our room [...] Each parcel that arrived caused an emotional
> outburst and floods of tears. We were not forgotten.
> Margarete Buber-Neumann, *Under Two Dictators*[24]

I also felt the presence of my family not far from me. News from them had often succeeded in crossing the isolation wall. One day, shortly after the Court of Appeals decided to close my case definitively, the penitentiary authorities came to the wing to make me sign a request which would allow me to seek political asylum in another country. This reminded me that my sisters continued their efforts to shorten my stay in prison.

Another day, a little time after the *coup d'état*, a big, clumsy soldier entered the wing. He walked between the two rows we were forced to form each time a soldier came, each of us in front of our cell, our backs turned to the aisle, and stopped next to me. Having verified my identity, he said that my family was doing fine and that they sent me their greetings. He turned around and left as he had come. Although we laughed at him and the incongruity of his attitude, it also seemed extraordinary to us. In the conditions which we were then in, this gesture had, indeed, great value and we, all the other prisoners as well as myself, were simply overjoyed. For me or anyone else, it was a message from the outside world. It showed that my mother and sisters were not far away, that they were just on the other side of the walls. I imagined my sisters going towards the soldier and asking him to pass on their greetings to their youngest sister. For a while, I almost had the impression of not being locked-up.

---

24. London, Victor Gollancz, 1949, p.133, translated by Edward Fitzgerald from *Als Gefangene bei Stalin und Hitler*, 1949.

On another occasion, in the middle of June, I was surprised when a soldier brought me a letter from my husband. It seemed like a miracle; I was unable to understand how or why it had reached me.

During the whole period of isolation in Córdoba, I clung fiercely to the memory of my family and my husband. Not only did I carefully erase what had happened during the months which preceded this period, but I embellished the image of my family as well as the role I played among them. During eight long months, I mentally drafted and deleted one thousand times the first letter I would write to them when we were allowed to correspond again. During all that time, I thought longingly of them. Every morning, while I paced my cell, I flew mentally towards the outside, towards them, towards all I missed so much and all I aspired to do once free. Every night I had long, vivid dreams; I dreamed about them, about freedom, about the beautiful things everybody wishes to have. I thought about the air, the sun, the countryside and the river; about our family gatherings as well as daily life. One of my cellmates from the opposite side of the corridor taught me how to sing a series of soulful songs which I performed for them with my eyes closed; I dedicated one of them to each family member. In this way, I shared with them songs, poems and memories. I felt that I was not alone. I always felt accompanied by their presence. When, some months later, we were finally able to correspond, the first letter from my sister went straight to my heart. I was touched by the resemblance of our feelings. I felt profoundly that I was not alone, that I had never been alone. It was as if they at home and I, locked in my cell, had constantly been communicating.

The presence of positive images in me was, in that situation of terror and isolation, a fundamental encouragement of a psychological order. Feeling my close relations next to me undoubtedly helped me to bear what was happening to us. My memory of them offered me the feeling of protection and security I needed. I felt I was near my people, near my city, near my family environment and near my maternal nest. Not only did I nourish the hope of finding them all soon, but also of making something better of my life with them.

XVII

> After the first day in the new ward, I began to go mad from the loneliness and the silence. I missed my ex-neighbours cursing and swearing, their middle-of-the-night howls for "just a bit of heroin" and their banging against the iron door for a light for a cigarette.
>
> Shirin Ebadi, *Iran Awakening*[25]

In December 1976, I was transferred with sixty-eight other prisoners to the prison at Villa Devoto in the province of Buenos Aires, where living conditions were less rough. It was one of the prisons that the regime had chosen as a showpiece for foreign observers. It was particularly intended to welcome the delegates of the international organizations who inspected places of confinement to ensure that human rights were being respected. This departure meant, nevertheless, that our situation would be prolonged. For months we had dreamed of freedom. The transfer, instead, although it meant the end of fright and isolation, distanced the idea of being released. An additional stay in a new prison deprived prisoner status of its temporary and random nature. Besides, the transfer, far away from my city, also meant being uprooted again.

We had waited for this departure for a long time. In September, a certain number of prisoners on the ground floor had already been transferred, and we knew that our turn would come soon. Any indication, any noise, took on large proportions. We speculated at great length on the alternatives and possibilities the military had reserved for us. All the other subjects of interest having gradually disappeared, the possibility of being transferred had become a subject of major importance. Knowing that we could be called to travel at any moment, we were watchful even during the night. In order to keep some of the garments we still had with us we left our trousers and shirts spread on the cement table,

---

25. *Op. cit.*, p.170.

one inside the other, ready to be put on quickly at the time of departure. However, despite our preparations, the announcement of the transfer took us by surprise and created great emotion. The order to leave the cell immediately and abandon all our possessions gave us no other option but to leave with what we had on.

By being transferred to Devoto, I was separated from all the companions of the Fringe. When I saw that my neighbour in cell No. 57, the companion whom I considered to be like a sister, with whom I shared our conversations in the afternoons, was still locked up, I understood that she would not be coming with us. She indeed did not belong to the list of prisoners to be transferred, and when she made her farewells from her cell she was deeply moved and cried. She put out her arm through the small window to give us her hand and tried to touch us for one last time. The emotion brought on by that hasty departure and the pain of the separation made us pull her arm so much on the uneven and sharpened window edge that it was cut and bled.

My other friend from the Fringe, the one that I admired most, had left some months earlier. The military had come to fetch her. They had already taken her once before to a concentration camp. It was she who, when she was back in the wing, had mentioned the existence of the "Boards of Recognition". She was twenty-eight-years-old and represented for me what I wanted to be ten years later, when I would be that age. I admired her intelligence and her understanding of things, and I set her up as a role model. When she was back from the concentration camp, she told my neighbour and I that she thought we were doing very well, and that of all the prisoners on the wing we were those who kept in the best state of mind and had the highest level of lucidity. If that was true, it is likely that the feelings we shared with one another, while talking during the afternoon hours, breaking the rules, had contributed to it. But true or not, her comment comforted me. Not only did I want to be a mature adult, as she was at that moment, but her judgment confirmed that I was on the right road. Her approval meant that I was still as I wanted to be. What I felt when she was taken a second time is not possible to define. I was completely ignorant of the reasons of her departure, but I do not remember having associated it with death. At no time did I think that she would be killed. At no moment did I think that she would either denounce or collaborate. It was like when one is sure to see something and, suddenly, the object disappears. Maybe it was disconcerting, maybe I had the impression that there were many things I did not understand, maybe it was even apathy. But her absence meant the loss of an important point of reference for me.

Our departure now also implied being taken away from the place where my family lived. That same day, just before the journey, I still had the occasion to feel their nearness. We had to wait for hours in a military airport, all in a row, heads lowered, eyes covered by bandages and hands fastened with wire behind our backs. The guards who watched us kept themselves busy by humiliating us. It seemed they made us sit and stand up without stopping as a way of killing time. Then, they forced us to move forwards and backwards. If we did not move quickly enough they dragged us by our clothes giving us a blow. But at a certain moment, I could see through the space left by the bandage with which my eyes were covered that a man was standing near me. In a low voice, he said to me that my mother greeted me and that all my family were doing well. I felt my throat tighten with emotion, but I had to keep my head down, not to move and not to show the least reaction. Once again, my mother and my sisters let me know that they were moving heaven and earth in order to get me out of prison. This person who had approached me, impeccably dressed as I could judge from his shoes and from what I could see of his trousers, no doubt participated in the military operations or was in collusion with them, but his presence next to me became suddenly cordial and warm. In spite of what he really represented, at that moment, this man made me feel a kind of paternal protection.

The penitentiary staff at Córdoba Prison also presented a kind of familiarity, and among the guards were the good and the bad ones, those with whom we had a good relationship and those we distrusted. There was a female guard who was particularly pleasant to us. One evening, I spoke to a soldier and explained to him that we needed to go to the toilet more often. He answered that he had not urinated since early that day. This guard, standing behind him, without being seen, threw out her chest and hardened the muscles of her arms as a mockery of what this soldier claimed as a sign of virility. Every evening when she came to lock us up in our cells, I explained my obsession for something sweet. One of those evenings, when she was locking my door, and in spite of the fact that she was herself meticulously checked as she entered the prison, she threw a toffee into the cell. In Devoto, instead, even these apparently banal details no longer existed. The guards all looked exactly the same: severe and indifferent. As for the women who accompanied us during our movements inside the prison, they were enormous and had a frightening appearance.

XVIII

> He does not yet know that it is better to be beaten, because one
> does not normally die of blows, but one does of exhaustion, and
> badly, and when one grows aware of it, it is already too late.
>
> Primo Levi, *If This is a Man*[26]

The journey from Córdoba to Villa Devoto lasted almost twenty-four hours and was hard. When we finally arrived at the penitentiary, before dawn, we were allowed to use the toilet. That was our first opportunity to do so since drinking the last *mate* in the prison, nearly a day earlier. In order to relieve the urgency of our need, we surrounded each of the latrine holes in groups of five. There, squatting, we all urinated desperately at the same time. The guards hastened us to finish, but it was physiologically impossible to obey. Then we were taken to an immense room which acted as a church. We passed from one corner to another of the room, as prison staff carried out the administrative tasks involved in our admission procedures. Under the gaze of the guards, we had to undress again for medical examination. We had to remain standing there for hours, always with lowered heads and hands behind our backs. Puddles of urine were noticed on the floor. Despite being allowed to go to the toilet when arriving in the morning, and that our body had not got any liquid since the morning of the previous day, some prisoners could not refrain, no matter how hard they might try, from peeing on their frocks.

At mid-day, two other prisoners and I were separated from the whole group and taken to Wing 37. This was a communal wing; there were no individual cells as in Córdoba. Some days later, we were transferred to Wing 34, very similar to this previous one. Inside the wing there were two rows of bunk beds separated by an aisle down the middle. On the

---

26. *Op. cit.*, p.155.

left of the door, there was a cubbyhole with three latrines, and on the right, three showers and the washbasin. The window, on the opposite side of the wing, was a narrow opening along the wall, almost at the top, out of our reach. In this space, up to twenty-five prisoners co-existed. When we arrived, twenty women already occupied the wing. They had, in their turn, been transferred shortly before from La Plata Prison, in the province of Buenos Aires. They welcomed us warmly and with plenty of affection. They immediately offered us a portion of cheese. Cheese! We could not believe what we were seeing! Besides, twenty-eight hours had passed since our last liquid breakfast taken before our departure from Córdoba.

We had come from a prison that had been a theatre of atrocities. The military had imposed inhuman treatment on us and had committed brutalities that violated any legislation. For months, nobody outside the prison knew what our fate was. For us, meeting these new prisoners gave us the first opportunity to speak about what we had experienced. Believing that one day we would be able to recount what we were going through helped us to bear the unbearable. It was our way of dealing with our isolation from the world and of protecting our humanity; it was our way of feeling we were united with those who were outside and of sharing our life with those whose memory helped us to survive. Now, however, that I could see this possibility, I felt alone, really alone, without anybody to share the world with as I thought. The story I offered my new companions at Devoto was not true in the eyes of the companions who had arrived with me from Córdoba. It was obvious that I did not tell stories with enough cruelty in them for a member of the People's Revolutionary Army. I felt embarrassed by her need to amplify the narration of experiences that were already terrifying. In addition, she criticised me severely for the type of letters I had written to my family.

After more than eight months of isolation, we were moved on, finally being able to exchange news with our families. In our excitement, we shared our mail with other companions, the letters which came in as well as those that went out. In my first letters to my family, instead of speaking about the drama that we had just lived out in Córdoba, I preferred to emphasise all the positive aspects that I could identify at that moment around me. Among other domestic details of our new life, I expressed my pleasure at eating pasta, which at that moment seemed to taste good although it was very prosaic. It was actually similar to a hard pâté, but I found it delicious compared with the aqueous dishes which had been served so frequently in Córdoba. Indeed, most of the time, the latter consisted of a reddish liquid in which — in the best of cases — vermicelli swam, and we were fortunate if we found a bone to gnaw on.

But in one of my letters, I also explained, although it may seem paradoxical, that in Córdoba, the food did not have a bad taste and that we ate a lot, which was indeed not wholly untrue. What actually happened was that we ate very badly. For endless hours, our stomachs were empty and when the bread finally arrived we devoured it. We did the same with the meals. Frequently it consisted mostly of a watery gruel which did not calm our hunger at all and it was even worse on cold days. As the last prisoners to be served received only the gravy, the guards took the precaution of beginning on different floors every time, something that made the uneven distribution fairer. At other times, fortunately, the dishes were more plentiful and there was enough food for all the prisoners on the three floors to have sufficient. We then compensated by eating three times more than when we received mostly liquid. If I had said that we did not eat enough, I would not have known how to explain that the prisoner who had put on the least weight had nonetheless gained six kilos. But at the time, perhaps I did not know how to express these nuances, and my story was badly interpreted by the young woman who had arrived with me.

This companion also considered that it was a mistake to emphasise the positive aspects of the new conditions of life in Devoto. Although in my letter I said that hygiene was not good, that bathrooms were small, dilapidated and unhealthy, and that it had been unpleasant to wake up in the middle of the night with serious bedbug stings, I had immediately added that I was glad to be able to take a warm shower in the morning, after so many months of being forced to take an ice-cold shower. I also wrote that we were lucky to be able to go to the toilet whenever we wished. After the months of deprivation and prohibition in Córdoba, it seemed luxury to me. Moreover, my main preoccupation was that my family knew that I was doing well, but for this companion it was as if by saying something relatively positive I had embellished the image of those who caused us so much pain. It was as if the main objective had been, not to demand justice from them, but to underline their cruelty. In the final analysis, her gesture judged people for what one believes they are and not for what they actually do; a gesture whose logical conclusion is not to prevent the action by condemning it, but to eliminate the person who commits it.

The same companion had already severely scolded me during the flight from Córdoba. We had had our hands lashed behind our backs, eyes bandaged over and heads bowed with no possibility of raising them for more than eighteen hours. The wait before take-off and after landing was horribly long. Seated on the floor of the military plane, legs crossed in the lotus position, I told myself that if I raised my head I would receive a blow, but at least I would have managed to loosen my cervical vertebrae for two seconds, something which seemed fundamental at the time. The blow, which I did indeed get, hurt me less, and the memory of it was less impressive than the reprimand this companion gave me because I had given the guards the chance to mistreat me.

But except for these unpleasant aspects, I accepted my new life with enjoyment and even excitement. In this wing, the prisoners were particularly affectionate and kind. In one of my first letters to my sisters, I spoke about my new companions in positive terms. Unlike at Córdoba Prison prior to the *coup d'état*, where even aspects of the everyday life, such as meals, management of the staff store or cleaning, took place according to our political affiliation, here we shared everything. Furthermore, this new life, compared to the one that we had just left, seemed magnificent to me from every point of view. Nevertheless, this optimism lasted only a few days, time to experience the emotion of meetings and to spend a good part of my time writing letters to my family.

XIX

> Nobody can live only according to himself. Thousands of fibres bind us to the others; among those fibres, like links of sympathy, our actions transmute themselves in causes and return to us under the shape of effects.
> Herman Melville

In my letters to my mother and my sisters, I especially tried to reassure them. I let them know that I was doing well and that I was impatient to have them visit. We were finally going to see each other again! I yearned to do so and I hoped that they would come quickly. As I was fearful that my mother would be horrified by the rundown condition of the building, since it was even more hideous than the one she had visited me in in Córdoba, I wanted to prepare her:

> In this prison, the building is of a very different kind from that of the prison of Córdoba. When one sees so many walls, so many bars, so much coldness and so much dilapidation, one does not feel necessarily well. But this is only the first impression, because afterwards, one puts all this aside and tries, above all, to feel well.

In this new prison, only members of our immediate family were allowed to visit us. When we arrived, we were permitted to see them in a small room where we could share our affection with them by touching each other through the bars. We did not know that these visits were a privilege compared with those in the glazed visiting rooms the authorities would impose later. At that time then, I thought it was important to minimise the effect of those bars interposed between us. When I wrote to my family, I showed enthusiasm and joy:

> This is not important, because the main thing is that we can see each other and speak and express what we have not been able to do for so long. We

shall also be able to hold each other's hands and give plenty of kisses to each other. Well, you can imagine how wonderful it will be!

The naïvety with which I tried to transmit optimism to my family by passing on a positive vision of my environment in my letters makes me smile today but, filled with conviction and spontaneity, this is indeed what I wrote when I was eighteen. Although life in prison extended for too long a period, I continued to look for the best every situation could offer me.

There were two kinds of visits. The communal visit was intended for families who lived in the surrounding areas. In the beginning, it took place on Friday: the same day, the men came in the morning and the women in the afternoon. But the frequency was reduced a few days after our arrival: from then on, visits took place every Monday and were alternate, one Monday for the women and the following one for men. As for the families who lived more than three hundred kilometres away, they had the right to a special visit every forty-five days. This consisted of six separate visits of one hour for six days in a row.

The support of my mother and my two sisters continued to be permanent and unconditional. They were always attentive to what was happening to me. They always made me feel their presence near me. In spite of the cost of travelling, they always came to see me. They always brought everything I asked them to. The documents they had to present to be allowed to enter the prison required more than one visit to State administrative departments and were difficult to obtain. However, they never skimped in their efforts, nor complained about the long hours of travel, or about painful waits in front of the door of the prison. As soon as I was transferred to Devoto, my elder sister, leaving her daily life behind, also moved to Buenos Aires to be closer to me. By doing so, she was able to attend the communal visit, which was more frequent than the special visit. Furthermore, in the capital, she would be able to take all necessary steps for me to be able to leave the country and to follow up the request I had signed in June when I was still isolated in Córdoba Prison.

On December 19th, she came to see me for the first time. That moment, the vision of which had lived in my spirit and fed my dreams for countless hours and days of isolation, finally arrived. We walked towards each other, hugged and kissed each other. The shared tenderness and emotion tempered the cold produced by the bars interposed between us. My first reaction was to ask where my husband was, to which she answered that he had left the country. I felt a profound disappointment that I suppressed at once. With regards to her own fears, I hurried to say that everything was alright. I imagined her worry since she had learnt that my husband had told me the story which so directly compromised her. While she insisted on the need to talk about it, I repeated that everything was alright. As for him, his leaving was maybe the most reasonable thing to do. But it is well-known that the heart has its reasons which reason knows nothing of, and I felt his departure as a new treason. Throughout the period of isolation in the cell at Córdoba, I had taken refuge in my memory of him and I imagined that he was waiting for me on the other side of the wall, which was not actually the case. It was as if, retroactively, I was deprived of the support I had leant on.

But that was not the only disappointment I would feel. On January 5th 1977, in the afternoon visiting time, returning from a walk in the yard, I heard somebody loudly shouting my name. When I recognised my father's voice, I wanted to shrink and disappear. I was too aware of the rules imposed inside the walls, and my father's behaviour frightened me. He was irritated because he could not see me. Being new in this prison, the guards had not succeeded in finding out which pavilion I was in, and while they were looking for me, visiting time was slipping by. I walked past the visiting room, lowered head and hands crossed behind my back, the posture we were forced to adopt whilst moving around the prison. Once inside the wing, I leaned against the door bars, my back turned to the external corridor; I closed my eyes and in a tired tone I said: "Father". I breathed deeply, I called the guard and told her that I was the prisoner they were looking for. When I was finally taken to the room where my father was waiting, I understood that such nervousness resulted from exhaustion. I learnt that, added to the difficulty in finding me, there were the hours of the journey that he had made during the night and then the wait, standing-up, outside the prison where he expected to be called to see me in the middle of the afternoon. But I tried all the same to make him understand that we were in a prison and that despite the fatigue he had to calm down.

When the visit reached its end, it appeared, logically, that the time which my father had been granted was much shorter than the statutory time, but visiting hours were collective, they began and ended for everybody at the same time, and they had to be respected. In spite of my explanations and my attempts to reassure him, he made a fresh scene. The next day, I waited for his second visit, but nobody came to fetch me. The mother of another prisoner let her know that my father had been deprived of his right to visit me for the five remaining days. One of my sisters told me later that, when he returned to Córdoba, he said nothing about what had happened during his visit. They had had difficulty collecting the money for his journey. I could do nothing else but sympathise with the humiliation which I supposed he must have felt. Furthermore, this situation opened old wounds. During the months of isolation in Córdoba Prison, I had built a mental relationship with my family, including my husband and my father, all living in harmony. To respond to my needs of that moment, I had forgotten that the latter had left home, abandoning all of us nine years earlier, that is, when I was nine. That day, reality struck me again, destroying my ideal world.

XX

> Nobody can gauge the violence of emotions who hasn't himself gone through the experience of loneliness among many thousands—and that in a concentration camp.
> Margarete Buber-Neumann, *Mistress to Kafka*[27]

As soon as the initial enthusiasm was over and the daily routine in the wing had been installed, I became aware of my political and ideological isolation. That was going to have an important effect on the development of our daily activities, but also on the attitude we would assume later with regard to the prison authorities. I had liked the fact that all the questions related to day-to-day problems of running the wing were handled in a collective way, and that we ate together. But apart from that, the prisoners, as in Córdoba, functioned according to their political affiliation. In this wing, there were three organizations, *Montoneros*, the People's Revolutionary Army and *Peronismo de Base* (the two former of which constituted the major extreme left-wing groups). Daily activities were developed within the framework of these organizations. Since I did not belong to any of them, and although I was still able to share recreation and discussions with their members, which I enjoyed, I had no other solution than to remain alone for a large part of the day while they met among themselves. Nevertheless, I remained active and I always found tasks to carry out or books to read. Besides, we could go outdoors into the yard again! If to uncover one's arms and to expose oneself to the sun after a long wintry period is pleasant, it is not difficult to imagine what one feels after staying in the shade for almost nine months. The first walks in the yard were, indeed, a source of enjoyment and happiness. I wrote to my sister:

---

27. *Op. cit.*, p.13.

> Every time I go out into the courtyard, I feel something very beautiful. It's as if the sun embraces me and enters me through the skin. I assure you that I do not exaggerate. It results from this huge need we have to feel these vital phenomena such as the air and the sun.

In this same letter, I told my sister that I had made many new acquaintances during these walks, and that I had been able to speak and exchange my experiences with prisoners from other wings. But it did not last long. On Christmas Day, prisoners of the major groups decided to sing partisan songs. Thereafter, we were punished and prevented from going out into the yard for five days. I could write to my family again after New Year's Eve:

> How did you spend Christmas and New Year's Eve? Very well, I suppose. So did we; especially Christmas Eve, during which we enjoyed ourselves; we were happy and emotional. As I had already told you, I dressed up as Father Christmas. You should have seen how beautiful it was. There were also very funny sketches. But from Christmas Day, the wings of the whole floor were punished for five days. That was because prisoners sang songs in the yard they did not have the right to sing. It can also have been the cause of my cold, because after five days without going out in the sun, five of us had a cold. We also had a good time at New Year's Eve, although it was not as good as that of Christmas. It was rather an evening of nervousness I would have wished to see over as quickly as possible. The wish I made for this year is to get back my dear freedom which I wish for so much and which we wish for everyone.

The nervousness caused by this experience in the yard marked the beginning of the degradation of relationships among the prisoners. My feelings changed, not with regards to any prisoner in particular, but to the policy dictated by the heads of the principal organizations. The differences and contrasts between our reactions to the measures taken by the prison authorities increased the tension among us and we grew apart from each other. Such different philosophies to deal with our situation isolated me even more. Consequently, during the largest part of day, I had nobody to share any activity with or even to speak to: in order to distract myself, I walked along the aisle, in between the two rows of beds. Sitting on those beds, the other prisoners chatted in endless whispers. In this environment, I waited with increasing impatience for my new request to leave the country to be approved. On February 2nd I wrote to my family:

> I don't know, I don't know, even though I make much effort to be calm, I don't succeed. I am sorry, but I don't succeed. Besides, sometimes I feel very alone. What can I say? The girls are very kind, we get on very well, they are affectionate, but I am always alone; then, I miss you. I miss you all. I am so impatient to take up a quiet life and to develop my daily activities in peace and with a regained serenity.

My solitude increased when my dear Isabel was taken away. We had become good friends. She was an activist of the *Peronismo de Base*, the smallest organization present in the wing. However, once their meetings ended, no political or doctrinal difference separated us. Isabel was important to me. She was sweet and pleasant. I laid across a bed, and she sat on the edge of the next bed, very close to mine, and made me put my head on her knees and massaged my temples. She was only two or three years older than me, but because of the way she spoke to me and treated me she made me feel her protection as if she had been much older. Our affection had been born for no visible reason. Of Isabel I only keep the image of her face and her gestures. Her skin was very white, almost transparent, her prominent nose betrayed her Italian origins and her hair was brown and quite short. We had not shared any secrets, and I never put a name to our relationship. I did not know where they took her, neither did I ever ask. I silently assumed the loss, almost without realising it, as if it had just been a new departure. Still now I wonder how it was possible and whether I am not romancing. Nobody mentioned her anymore, not even her closest companions within her organization. As though it was something they had better not speak about. Still now, when I recall it, I have a feeling of incredulity. I really never did hear of her being mentioned again. It is true that we were used to separations and to their unpredictable timing. But Isabel's disappearance left a huge void in me. Every murder committed inside or outside of the prison extinguished a little bit of my being, and when Isabel disappeared something in me disappeared as well.

Some time before, one of my companions on the wing had written a letter to me:

> Childhood still plays in each one of your gestures, in your smile, in the thousand small stars which shine in your eyes; I discover that I appreciate you, because you keep your joy, your laughter, this purity we had once upon a time and I do not know how or when we lost. We all have our beauty, and I believe that we have to offer it day after day; today I appreciate your simplicity, another day, something else that I discover in other companions. Then, don't let your joy to be extinguished, and all of us, let's create a different world and colour it with the beauty we all have in us…

But now I was alone. I had nobody with whom to elaborate my ideas, to tell my feelings to or to have a dialogue with. Not only was my adolescence reaching its end, but also the bases on which I had built my identity.

XXI

> Solitude encircles and engirdles him, always more threatening, more throttling, more heart-oppressing, that terrible goddess and mater saeva cupidinum[28] — but who knows nowadays what solitude is? ...
> Friedrich Nietzsche, *Human, All Too Human, A Book for Free Spirits* [29]

> One does not approach solitude without moral provisions.
> Honoré Balzac, *Madame de la Chanterie*

On Monday, February 21st 1977, the new visiting rooms were inaugurated. They consisted of a long row of cabins separated by a partition which ended above our heads, each one with two small tables, placed against each other and separated by a vertical pane. The visitor on one side, the prisoner on the other, could converse through a device which looked like two big ladles[30] joined by a tube allowing the voice to pass from one side of the pane to the other, in such a way that, by bringing the mouth close to the ladle to speak, then the ear to listen, the two people could try to communicate amid the inevitable hubbub of many voices talking at the same time.

The majority of prisoners refused the first visit. The leader of each of the two major organizations had indeed decided that their members would do this by way of protest against the new system imposed by the prison authorities. I evaded their order and accepted the visit. I went to speak to my sister through the pane. The difference from the visits in the small room where, on two or three occasions, we had been able to

---

28. In Latin in the text: Wild mother of the passions.
29. London, T N Foulis, 1909, p.6, preface by the author, translated by Helen Zimmern.
30. *In memoriam* Silvia Clementi whose communication with her young son was only allowed in this cabin once a week. Once, at his grandmother's, the child, rummaging through a box full of old stuff, found a handleless ladle. Walking through the garden, he showed his precious object while he said "Mum, mum".

see our families and touch each other through the bars was devastating. To see my sister and not to be able either to touch her or to speak to her spontaneously saddened me. We forced a smile and gazed at each other trying mutually to breathe confidence and optimism into each other. However, in our hearts, we recognised the oppressive reality of the situation: we had been separated; I was kept locked-up, removed farther and farther. Nevertheless, we could continue to see each other still.

When this visit ended, I was taken back to the wing. But a little later, the guard came to fetch me to take me to the legal department. In this office, we were normally informed of releases and departures abroad, generally known as the *option*. We opted to leave the country. But although this option was a right written into the national constitution, it was inconceivable for the Fascist mentality of the Argentine military who wanted to exert total power over us. This is why the first request—which I had made as soon as my case had been temporarily closed—had been automatically annulled the day the military took power, ignoring the constitution. Some time later, they established a parody of the right because they could, at any time, decide not to respect it. It was not a question of demanding one's "right to exclusion" any more, of being sent abroad without having the right to return to the country, but only of asking for authorisation to leave the country; and the military had the right to deny it. This is what they did with my second request, the one that my sisters had come to get me to sign in Córdoba Prison shortly after the *coup d'état*, ten months earlier.

Given that this request, which would allow me to travel to France, fell due on February 23rd, it was easy to suppose that I was being summoned to the legal department to be informed that, this time, it had been granted. Consequently, with my companions, we jumped for joy. By doing that, we certainly demonstrated one of the most important paradoxes provoked by authority: the pleasure some of its actions can produce in those against whom it is wielded. The impotence of my situation made it so that I could even be delighted to be cast away from my own country.

However, contrary to my expectations, the motive for this hearing was not to commute my sentence but rather to inflict an additional one on me. In the legal department, Jesús Galíndez, the head of security, was waiting for me. He accused me of scratching the small table in the visiting room where I had seen my sister. Without presenting any proof, he asked me to sign a denial. This gesture demonstrated, on the one hand, the immense powers that the prison authorities had over us and on the other the precautions they still had to take in legal terms. Mirroring a constitutional State, they granted me the choice of signing a statement in which I did not take responsibility for the offence. I never knew why they decided to punish somebody or why I was chosen.

If there was still any doubt about whether accepting the visit meant I was on the side of the prison authorities, this punishment dispelled that thoroughly incorrect notion. My only decision had been not to accept a measure of protest instigated by the majority groups, which I also refused to support. I had just taken advantage of the narrow window of opportunity I still enjoyed in such a situation: to accept or refuse the chance of seeing my family. And I had decided to accept. By differentiating myself from the vast majority of political prisoners, this action highlighted not only to what point I was isolated within the prison but also how far I had distanced myself from any kind of power, whatever it might be.

Already, in Córdoba Prison, I had opposed measures of protest the prisoners belonging to the majority groups had wanted to carry out. Among those measures, there was one proposal to pour an enormous pot of soup through the bars of the wing towards the outside. I do not remember exactly the reasons for it, but I can easily imagine that it was a way of protesting about the food we got, which as I described earlier was of bad quality. It does not matter in any way that the claim itself was more than justified; however, the act of protesting suggested by the prisoners was, at the very least, out of place. Indeed, in our conditions, it was easy to imagine that the military only needed a pretext to massacre us, or at least to justify new security measures and extreme sanctions. But at the time, in setting myself apart by this gesture, which was in some ways suicidal, I still enjoyed the position I shared with my independent companions of the Fringe. In Devoto, instead, I was the only one to differentiate myself from the majority inside the wing, and also I believed the only one in the whole prison. Consequently, the punishment I had just received from the authorities, after refusing to adhere to the measure of protest of the prisoners, added to the already increasing isolation caused by the internal organization and daily routine of the majority groups, from which those who did not belong were excluded. Internal isolation on the one hand, punishment from the authorities on the other, increased the impossibility of identifying myself with anyone; this powerlessness amplified my feeling of loneliness. In those circumstances, when I was locked-up in the cell in solitary confinement, it was difficult for me to hold on to any reason which would still justify my existence.

PART TWO
SOLITARY CONFINEMENT

All [the prisoners] kept their heads down, buried in their buttoned-up coats, and all were chilled to the bone, not so much from the actual cold as from the prospect of having to spend the whole day in it.

Alexander Solzhenitsyn, *One Day In The Life of Ivan Denisovich*[1]

---

1. Penguin Books, 1984, p.12, translated by Ralph Parker from *Odin den Ivana Denisovicha*, 1962.

Solitary

Nowadays there is only one cell where at the time there were two (as explained in *Chapter XXIII* on page 118). The former dividing wall has been demolished. I was in the cell on the right. The trace left on the floor shows the size of the space where I was kept for fifteen-and-a-half days. Between an iron board nailed to the wall which served as a bed, and the dividing wall, I could take just three steps. The spots on the floor show where the door of each cell was, which explains why I could put my arm through the small opening in the door and empty my pot, making an effort to aim at the latrine which can still be seen bottom right.

XXII

> [...] constant solitude is such a cruel torture for me that I'll never resist the need to produce some sound from my lungs, and ask my neighbour for an answer. And even if my neighbour were silent I'd address my words to the bars on my window, to the hills over there, to the birds flying past.
>
> Silvio Pellico, *My Prisons*[2]

Following the incident of the supposedly damaged table in the visiting room, I was taken directly from the legal department of Devoto Prison to solitary confinement on the fifth floor. *Chanchos*, pigs, that is what we called the punishment cells. While being taken up the stairs, my head lowered and hands cuffed behind my back, I told myself that my companions would not see me return to the wing, that, when my sister came to visit me, she would not be allowed to see me and that the letters for my family would not be sent.

No complaint would thwart the feeling of powerlessness that this new confinement caused me; a silent scream tightened my breast and hurt me. After so many changes of circumstance and difficult experiences, confronted by this new hardship, I felt such fatigue that I had no energy left to cling to any memory. I was far from everything and everybody. The mental image of my family and friends faded and the security that their presence had given me dissipated.

In any situation of danger, abandonment or suffering, we cling to the idea of getting some assistance; but when I was going to be locked away alone again in a cell, reality cruelly blocked any hope in this direction. During my stay in prison, I had gone through different phases. I had adapted to the simplest ones as well as to the most complex. In each of them, I had managed to overcome, to find a new balance and make sense of what I was experiencing. Generally, I had shown myself equal to the

---

2. *Op. cit.* p.136.

task. The situation we had gone through in Córdoba Prison had truly tested our resistance. Everything had been extremely difficult. However, thanks to the presence of my companions, the eight months without any contact with the outside world had not altered my psychological or moral integrity, neither did they make me lose consciousness of who I was. After my arrival at Devoto Prison, I wrote in one of my first letters to my family that the last weeks had been tough and difficult to bear:

> I had to make a big effort not to lose my spirits […] I had to remain lucid to think clearly. The last period was difficult, it was hard, I assure you.
>
> Let me tell you that from the beginning, I always wanted to see you again. Then, when I thought of you, a profound emotion invaded my body. As you did not know anything of what we were living, I thought that this must not be easy for you (as well as for all the families in this same situation). I imagined that Mom would be very worried and would feel sick. Then, every time I thought of her or of all of you, my lips drew into a big smile which expressed my wish to see you soon and tell you that I was doing fine, that you did not have to worry, that I loved you and that I was going to do my best to continue to do well.

But it had hardly been three months since we had had that experience where each of us had been locked-up alone practically all day. If that had wounded me, this new isolation rubbed salt into the wound. The first time, I had lived it day after day, without really thinking about what would follow, and I had easily managed to adapt my reaction to every situation. But having left the cell where I had been locked-up for such a long time, it was not easy to stop myself from being seized by anxiety.

In my second letter to my family from Devoto Prison, I told them that I felt very well, but that my wellbeing was not guaranteed:

> I'm very calm; I can do things quietly and with serenity. It's as if I can rest after having lived through a very tough situation. I don't know, sometimes I'm afraid that my calm will not last long […] After I arrived here, I was able to relax. This new situation is less restrictive; but after a while (after the

emotion of all the visits), I began to feel very nervous: I felt I had a weight which could not be lifted and which I could not share with anybody. I then decided not to repress it any longer, and it was as if I had released the reins: my nervousness dissolved. Then, I was able to unburden myself and one day I cried; by doing so, I released all the accumulated tensions.

But when I saw that I was to be locked away again, alone in a cell, in a wing where there was nobody, I did not have the force to resist so much cruelty. The idea of again experiencing a similar situation made me lose my balance. The flash of this recollection blinded me, and powerlessness awoke in me a feeling of despair. A stream of sensations that, at the beginning, I had not consciously faced, returned to my memory. Before, I had repressed them, in order to face up to the circumstances we had to endure; I had hidden them between two ideas which my consciousness had assembled to give coherence to thought and to face the reality. But now that I was confronted with the same ordeal again, they came to the surface and my senses were defeated.

Solitary

XXIII

>...what's the meaning of days, when time is no longer counted by hours and minutes, only by heartbeats?
>Margarete Buber-Neumann, *Mistress to Kafka*[3]

>One of the worst features of German concentration camps was that no term was fixed for release. That "not knowing how long" was one of our worst tortures.
>Margarete Buber-Neumann, *Under Two Dictators*[4]

Time can only be measured by what has happened previously and by what can happen later. On my arrival on the fifth floor, without understanding what had just happened, and without knowing what would come later, I had the impression that time had stood still. When I was accused of scratching the small table, I was so stunned that I did not dare ask what fate was reserved for me, or how long my punishment would last. Not to know the length of my confinement prevented me from realising that my reality would ever undergo the least change. Once in the cell, I felt immensely lonely. There was no-one to tell that I did not want to be locked-up again, or to ask why it was happening.

Two years had gone by since the police came to fetch me at home and locked me up for the first time in the cell of the police station in Río Cuarto. But during all that time, I had been in touch with people. Here instead, on the fifth floor of Devoto Prison, the isolation was complete, and events so non-existent that it was impossible to anticipate anything. In this new cell, there were no humiliations or ill-treatment such as we had been subjected to in Córdoba Prison, but the companions with

---
3. *Op. cit.*, p.16.
4. *Op. cit.*, p.212.

whom I had borne them were present no more. The other cells were empty, and moreover, although the door of my cell had a small opening, it did not allow me to see the wing. The fifth floor consisted of groups of two cells, in front of which was a small common space with a latrine on one side and a sink on the other, separated again from the large corridor by another solid door.

But even if I had not been through so many ordeals since being arrested and locked-up for the first time, the sensation I had when I arrived in this new, deserted wing, and the void I discovered in this cell from where I could see nothing, would have been enough to make me fall into a state of instability. Although the prison was such an enormous building that prisoners could not figure out using their imagination, in the penitentiary at Córdoba I still knew where I was. I had arrived during the day, I could raise my head, and my eyes were open; then I had been able to look around me. I knew where each of my steps took me and I had been able to track down where our wing was. Furthermore, from our cells, we could still look towards the world outside through the windows which, although they had been designed according to high security regulations, were still open. So, the noises of the area and the voices of the children playing in the street still reached us. The prison was no less a prison, and the last vision which we had was the wall of the penitentiary. But in Devoto, we did not even have this vision.

In this new establishment, it was rare to hear noises from outside. Not only had we arrived there at night, with bandaged eyes, but once inside we had to move around with lowered heads. When we were transferred from one place to another within the prison, the prohibition on looking around prevented us from having an idea of where we really were. In the wing, it was impossible to look outside. Day or night, whatever the weather, thunderstorm or rain, a sunny or cloudy day, it made little difference to us. The lack of contact with natural changes and the ban on wearing a watch altered our relationship to time. During the months of isolation in Córdoba, similar factors had already affected my mental state. In this punishment cell, in addition to the lack of reference to time and place, there was a total absence of human and social contact.

XXIV

> Only now did I realise how diabolically ingenious [this] method was, how fiendishly well devised in psychological terms. In a concentration camp you might have had to cart stones until your hands bled and your frost-bitten feet fell off in your shoes, you would have slept packed together with two dozen other people in the stench and the cold. But you would have seen faces, you could have stared at a field, a cart, a tree, a star, something, anything, while here you were always surrounded by the same things, always the same, always the terrible same. There was nothing here to distract me from my thoughts, my delusions, my morbid recapitulations.
>
> Stephan Zweig, *Chess*[5]

The image of people who surround us or we knew or saw in the past, or that, real or imaginary, we would like to meet some day, permanently visits our thoughts. When we are alone, we call on them. We mentally return to our last dialogue with those people, we tell them what we did not say when we were talking to them, but that, we now think, we should have said; we exchange our opinions, sometimes we even argue or we get angry and quarrel with them; we show ourselves the images they left us again and again; we project ourselves into the future we would wish to share with them then. In short, we produce and reproduce relationships with others in an imaginary way, and it prevents us from feeling lonely.

But in this cell, who could I call on? Who could I appeal to? Nobody inhabited my mental space anymore. In this cell, I lacked absolutely everything that had made me somebody. When I was imprisoned, I had been separated from all those I loved, from all those with whom I shared my life. The military had savagely isolated us. Because she was not part of my family, my best friend and comrade from the party I belonged to

---

5. *Op. cit.*, pp.40–1.

could no longer write to me. So many other comrades had had to hide. My husband had gone abroad. The prisoners from the Fringe in Córdoba Prison were no longer with me. The political isolation in Devoto had finally condemned me to be alone. For two months, since my arrival in this new prison, I had spent most of the time walking up and down the aisle on my own. When the major organizations considered it necessary to refuse visits, I alone had made the decision to accept them. Furthermore, the period of detention had become long, too long. Although my mother and sisters showed me all their affection and support, as the weeks had gone by, I no longer knew what to tell them in the letters I wrote to them from this new prison:

My adored sister,

Your letter is very beautiful and absorbing. You let me know about everything happening outside and allow me to keep in touch with the world; with this small but big world, which is our home, as well as with this beautiful city, which is Córdoba.

The card you sent me is very beautiful. It is very joyful, and its contents are very moving. You write beautiful things, which fill my soul. After reading your letters, I feel fine, very fine. I feel a great calm and a deep peace. In short, please, write often to me; it fills me with happiness. I am going to write to you and we shall be good friends by mail. Even though sometimes I find that I do not have many things to tell you. What can I say? Here, the possibilities of change in the course of the day are tiny.

When I receive your letters as well as the visits from our eldest sister I feel happy and satisfied. Incredible as it may seem, these things have a huge influence on my mood. This week I've been a little bit sad and tired. Here, when one feels the morale going down, one has to gather all one's forces to pull oneself up, because the environment gives us very little help to allow us to lift ourselves out of this state. One has to think that there's only oneself and the companions around us. From there, it is necessary to know how to gather all our courage to bear the bad moments, so that they don't press down on our spiritual, mental and moral integrity. I think that this is a constant, slow and sometimes hard learning process.

Goodbye lovely. I love you very much and I expect you to come very soon. We shall speak again and again. Say hello to all the friends and dear ones from me. Bye, bye, one thousand kisses.

Your little sister.

Shortly after I was put in solitary confinement, it was difficult for me to imagine the real existence of people, a world, time and space outside my small square. People disappeared from my mind, even those who I knew, and who consequently I would see again. I had no social references anymore, I neither found an answer to my questions nor anybody who I could ask them of, I could see nothing or nobody in front of me; then, I could no longer keep perspective, I could not relate to what I was undergoing, in brief, it was impossible for me to project myself into the future and think that my solitude was caused by the punishment and was, therefore, only momentary. My solitary confinement acquired a total and absolute dimension. If confinement is objectively always confinement in itself, I experienced this one in a completely different way from the previous ones. In contrast to those, I could see no end to my new situation.

Solitary

XXV

> Open up! Open up there! I'll take them all, the boots, the tongs, the molten lead, the tweezers, whatever you've got! I want some real suffering! Let's have a thousand gashes, let's have the acid and the whips, anything but this pain! Anything but this tickling that never hurts enough!
> Jean-Paul Sartre, *No Exit*[6]

When I was in the cell at the police station in Río Cuarto — where I had been locked-up when arrested — I knew that I had escaped torture. When I say torture, I mean blows and ill-treatment of a physical kind. In a system where the torturers applied electric shock treatments to inmates' genitals, where they kept prisoners' heads immersed in water or urine for what seemed like an eternity, when they covered their faces with plastic bags filled with excrement, and where they hit them with brutality; in a system where the torturers sexually abused women with savagery and complete impunity, it was hard to consider as torture a detention of ten days in a cold and empty cell, accompanied by some threats uttered during interrogations.

The expression I saw on the face of the prisoners on my arrival at Córdoba Prison had also allowed me to understand my privilege at not having been tortured. At *Bon Pasteur*, when Mother Superior had informed me of my transfer, I had had the time to get ready for the journey and properly dressed. Although I had spent the night in a niche of cement at the police station, the next day I still looked impeccable. That was also a peculiarity I had developed after listening to the stories my mother told me when I was a child about my grandfather and Swiss soldiers during the First World War, as was my ability to sleep on hard stone. Consequently, when I arrived at the penitentiary, I had the aspect — as one of my companions told me later — of one of the *petit bourgeoise*: a fair-haired

---
6. London, Samuel French Inc., pp.47–8, adapted by Paul Bowles from *Huis Clos,* 1945.

Solitary

girl with white shoes and well-groomed hair, tied-up in a ponytail. I did not correspond, as I learnt later, to the stereotype of the beaten-up political prisoner who arrived at the prison after a stay in the Centre of Information,[7] the place opposite the beautiful colonial cathedral in the centre of Córdoba, where torture was usually carried out.

But the punishment to which I was subjected in this new cell was of a much more subtle nature than threats or blows applied directly to my body: now, it was solitary confinement. I was left alone. Having imagined, with all my companions in the wing, that I would be freed soon, in a split second my universe had narrowed again. It did not become anything other than this cold and empty space, where my only alternative was to remain sitting or stretched out on the iron bed or to take three steps. Since the cell was quite new, there was not even a drawing on the wall which my brain could fix on; not even a quote left by a non-political prisoner who would have been there before me; no heart with two names which would have inspired me to imagine a love story; none of those naughty sentences, the fruit of exuberant popular creativity which would have made me laugh. The void was new, impeccable. There wasn't even any flaw or imperfection on the wall on which to fix my attention; not even a spot on which I would have been able to discover forms with which to play mentally.

Apart from the four walls, the small windows above, the door and the metal plate nailed to the wall, which served as a bed, there was nothing in this cell. I never heard the sound of voices. I was forbidden to speak to the guard, or to look at her. When she opened the door for me to take the mattress in or out, to go to the toilet, or to pick up a meal, she forced me to do everything head bowed and very quickly. My senses were deprived of any stimulation. I had been left alone: alone, faced with myself, this person I could not even see. No face in front of me, not even an object to reflect mine. Nothing, nothing, nothing. There was nothing to do, nothing to listen to, nothing to look at. And since I did not know how long I would stay there, I could not even project myself forward in time

---

7. Where the Memorial Museum of Córdoba now is.

towards the end of this torture. The void and the nothingness reigned around me. What could I do to prevent them from dominating me?

If we think about it, there is nothing in life which oppresses us more than the sensations brought on by the threat of nothingness. We would do anything to escape it. Life can of course continue to unfold without reference to the void of nothingness, and indeed, with many of our actions we often try to deny that this is our only and ultimate fate. However, the only means of surviving it is to take our bearings from life, whatever form it takes. Think about it. The fear caused by nothingness makes sanity explode. The threat of nothingness dominates us. It is stronger than any will, any intention. Nothing subverts our decisions more easily than the impossibility of resisting the threat of nothingness. There is no determination to oppose it, no mental structure against it, no human theory that can withstand it.

The threat began as soon as I got up in the morning. At six o'clock, I had to take the mattress out into the corridor. From that moment on, I had to organize my day. In order to understand what I felt, readers should imagine themselves in a situation in which they wonder each moment what they will do just afterwards, without even being able to know how long this uncertainty will last. Those who read this book will take some hours to finish it; they may read some pages, put the book aside, dedicate themselves to other activities and resume reading later. It will then be difficult for them to imagine the passage of time in which there is nothing to do, where nothing can happen. How do I expect them to understand, if I, who lived it, cannot explain it? How do I describe the power exerted by this small vacuum on my soul, when my eyes could settle only on the walls, on the ground, on the door, on the small window above, on the holes of the plate of metal which was used as a bed?

What did I think about during all that time? What kind of connection did I give to my thoughts? Who did I exchange my ideas with? How did I compensate for the devastation caused by the threat of the nothingness and to recover the place it took?

For many years, I thought that I would never be able to approach these subjects. The impossibility of describing the void and the nothingness was a real obstacle. I appealed to theories which I thought would help to explain it. I appealed to well-read people who seemed to have the necessary intellectual skill. I imagined that their knowledge and their experience would allow them to give me some advice, that their comments would help me to build this story which I knew well, but I did not know how to present at all. In the end I did what some authors do: live certain experiences to be able to speak better about them. Then, I tried to re-live what I had gone through. On more than one occasion, the sadness awoken by solitude seemed to encourage me to go farther and reach into the nothingness again. But it was impossible, there was always something which prevented me from doing it… I could get up, walk and move to another room; I could fix my glance on another object, go to the toilet, take a shower; I could carry out a domestic task, flick through a book; I could eat something or boil some water to make tea, caress my dog or think of going out in the street. The idea of taking some action was enough to remove me from the nothingness. I had no other solution but to bear the suffering caused by being lonely; but the nothingness, I have never found it again.

In this cell, on the other hand, I had no possibility of imagining that I could carry out the most insignificant of activities, apart from walking… and counting. This habit, which I had already adopted in Córdoba, became the greater part of my routine. For hours alone with myself, figures often replaced ideas, they absorbed them, helped them to disappear. They occupied my spirit and emptied it. I counted the holes of the patch on which I slept in all the possible ways, vertically, horizontally and diagonally. I divided the bedplate in two, then, into smaller portions; I separated it into triangles, I created small groups of three or four holes, or more, I imagined geometrical images; I even ventured as far as to create star designs. I also counted the bars of the small window. There were two. And I finally counted the three steps with which I could cross my cell. I walked without stopping, until it made my head spin. Faster every time. I counted my steps in both directions. I walked for an incalculable length of time. In the meantime, the light of my eyes went out, taking with it any sign of interest. I was far from everybody; I was even far from Córdoba, where in spite of the horror the presence of the others saved me from nothingness.

XXVI

> I [...] filled in the nothingness which menaced me by eating my bread. This broke the spell and calmed the animal gnawing at my solar plexus.
>
> Christopher Burney, *Solitary Confinement* [8]

> Starch. O starchy foods, my sadness, my companions, my visitors, my compulsory menu, my survival, my personal abomination, my worn-out burned-up tossed-aside love, my ration of calories, my obsessive madness! Starches that I eat and pass through my stomach with something like pleasure.
>
> Tahar Ben Jelloun, *This Blinding Absence of Light* [9]

If nothingness threatened my mental world, my physical state did not help to combat it. Since I had been arrested and taken to Río Cuarto Police Station, where my body had already been weakened as a consequence of the cold and the bad food, my health had only got worse. In the new punishment cell, my body barely accepted any food and quickly got rid of it. I had trouble swallowing, even the bread. In Córdoba Prison it had become the measure of confinement and solitude we suffered. If we had some bread left for breakfast, it depended on what had happened the previous day. The more the soldiers shut us in our cells, the more the result of their interventions in the prison became serious, the less was the possibility that our bread would last until the next day. We ate it with greediness. In this situation, where we did nothing all day, we longed for bread at any time. Anxiety, nervousness, fear, enjoyment, boredom, everything was accompanied by bread. It seemed to work as a palliative to the effects of the terror sown by the military. It

---
8. London, Macmillan & Co Ltd, 1961 [1952] p.21.
9. London, Penguin Books, 2005, p.34, translated by Linda Coverdale from *Cette Aveuglante Absence de Lumière*, 2001.

was an anxiolytic as well as a symbol of life. But confronted with a new confinement, I could accept it no more.

Then, hunger was chronic. During the night, I dreamed about food, and during the day I was obsessed by it. But, nevertheless, I did not want to eat any more. The bread I got in the morning was my only solid meal of the day. Very often I refused it; at other times I kept it but I gave it back to the guard afterwards. Indeed, accepting the meal had as bad an effect on me as refusing it. Lunch was extremely bad: since the solid part of the meal settled on the bottom of a cylindrical, narrow but very high jar, and since I had no ladle to get at it, except a small metal jar, all that I could retrieve was a liquid of reddish colour with a part of the layer of fat which floated on the surface. I had the choice between not drinking it and increasing my hunger, or drinking it and, upset by the sickness or the cramps of my stomach, calling the guard loudly until she deigned to open the door to allow me to go to the toilet. In both cases, I found myself with nothing in my stomach, tormented by a sensation of being lightheaded and mental emptiness; I then bent down to collect the breadcrumbs scattered on the floor.

In the morning, when I was given *mate*, I got it in the same jar in which I had previously urinated. The opportunities to go to the toilet were restricted and depended on the willingness of the guard. Fortunately, I had realised that if I put my arm out through the small window of the door and aimed well, the contents of the jar fell exactly in the hole of the latrine situated outside the cell. For this, I needed to keep the jar I had been given for breakfast with me without the guard noticing this. But this operation only resolved one major problem. There was another inconvenience: I never managed to drink the *mate* while it was warm. Indeed, since the jar was made of metal, it took the temperature of the liquid. If the *mate* was warm, the edge of the jar burnt my lips. If I waited until it was cool, the *mate* cooled at the same time.

Sitting or lying on the bed, which was actually a metal board nailed to the wall, I moved constantly to alleviate the pain in my hip bones, my shoulder blades or my pubis as they rested on the multiple holes which lined it at regular intervals over its whole surface. I was becoming so bony that the different parts or my skeleton felt as though they were being cut by the edges of these holes.

After a few days, the blouse I was wearing when I had been locked-up in solitary confinement tore from top to bottom. Thus, my back was directly exposed to the air, to the cold of the iron and to the fleas I saw jumping from time-to-time. With so much discomfort, my state of desolation increased. My body lost its energy and decreased in weight and volume. The image of people gradually disappeared from my mind; my eyes emptied. Then I walked, ceaselessly, three steps in one direction, three steps in the other; I endlessly counted them, on and on, as if it were an attempt not to give up.

In previous situations, I had kept a link with others and with the changing world, and that had allowed me to feel fine. Two months earlier, I had written to my family expressing all the gratitude I felt towards them and my friends: "I would never know how to thank you enough for what you did for me and for the tranquillity you offered me during all this time." I had written to my mother not to worry, that "I will do my best so that my smile never fades from my lips". I had added that, during the previous months, I had feared I could have hardened in those circumstances, but that nevertheless, "I have never stopped laughing or playing on every single occasion that came along." But there, in that cell, solitude transformed the cold, the hunger, the fatigue, the disease, the decline, the silence, the uncertainty and the desolation into torture, physical and moral, whose ultimate purpose was to break any link with reality.

Torture succeeded in isolating me, in separating me completely from my people, in making me feel that I did not exist any longer. It did not only try to hurt me or to make me speak, but on the contrary, to silence me, to destroy me, making me feel that I was no longer human, until I had the feeling of not belonging to the human race any more, until I was in a state where the only voice I heard was that of solitude.

Solitary

XXVII

> And why should I be ashamed, in the dread moment when my whole existence is trembling between being and not being, when the past is gleaming like lightning over the dark abyss of the future, when everything around me is falling away and the world crashing to ruin over my head?
>
> Johann Wolfgang von Goethe, *The Sorrows of Young Werther*[10]

One day, tired of taking three steps one way and three steps the other, I lay on the iron ledge which served as a bed. Deep in a crushing solitude which would last I knew not how long, I felt desperately abandoned. No longer having the memories of those who I had shared my life with until then, of those who were like me and whose company inspired my confidence and safety, I stopped being what I was. I became incapable of reproducing meetings or mental dialogue, in which I saw myself as I had previously done. I saw myself, not as I would have liked to, but as others saw me. First of all, I was discussing matters with my companions from Manuel Belgrano College. It was at the end of classes, at mid-day. We stood near the stone benches on one side of the big square at the entrance. I was talking to other classmates. Pablo was one of them. But I did not see myself in discussion with them. I saw myself as they saw me. I was unable to reproduce the speech I would have given as an activist of a leftist party. They also were activists from the left, but from another organization. They belonged to the youth section of one of the two major extreme left-wing organizations in the country. Pablo and his friends belonged to the UES — High School Students Union. I belonged to the FAES — High School Students Anti-imperialist Front — *Vanguardia Comunista*. During our discussions, listening to the others was not as important as arguing what we thought

---

10. The Scholartis Press, 1929, pp.8–9, translated by William Rose from *Die Leiden des Jungen Werthers*, 1774.

was important to say and that we had forcibly learnt from those who thought as we did.

Everything happened in my imagination. In my discussions with Pablo and his companions, I would have remembered my own companions and friends. It was only thanks to them that I could exist, maintain a position and be somebody in the eyes of others. But now, all the scenes of dialogue seemed so distant that I could not conjure up anybody in my imagination to prompt me. At college when I discussed issues with the activists of the other left-wing organizations, I held coherent views on policy and an attitude I shared with my companions in the party. But now, they were not there. Furthermore, to face a new reality which surpassed the imagination, any known discussion would have been insufficient. It would have been necessary to create a new one, and dialogue, by definition, requires two participants. Consequently, no discussion could describe the suffocation I felt in this cell.

These students with whom I discussed things were in my mind on their own. I was no longer there to continue to discuss matters with them. It was not I who imagined them speaking to me. It was they who spoke inside me. It was they who saw me in a way I had never seen myself before. Their presence in me offered me neither company nor safety; on the contrary, it constantly shook me violently. They mocked me and laughed, they ridiculed the values and ideas I sought to defend and which had set me apart from them; their harassing weakened the strength which I had employed to differentiate myself from them. Maybe they represented their companions who, inside the prison, mocked me because, instead of joining them, their politics and their measures of protest, I had accepted the visit and I had been punished all the same.

Whatever it was, suddenly, it was not only companions of the Manuel Belgrano College who criticised me, but many others. My mind filled with hostile faces that berated me. Their images whirled around in my head; my ideas became muddled, collided with each other, quarrelled among themselves. I do not know which chain of thought led me to this mental turn around, but I saw a thousand faces attacking me. It was as if the features of all those I had rejected in my daily life, those I had opposed, those whose opinions I had not accepted, those whose existence I had not recognised, had appeared to me in chaos. These were apocalyptic images of people who, using my own language, questioned me and judged me. Confronted by them, alone, deprived of the presence of any familiar and friendly image to defend me, I felt defeated. The severity of their comments led to the destruction of my being. The barriers and usual limits of existence collapsed and the force I had always displayed to differentiate myself from the others weakened. The image and the opinion I had of myself faded. Everything which had seemed important to me in my life until then collapsed. I was ashamed of all the acts which day-by-day had built my identity, and which, by hiding behind it, found justification. I felt ridiculous for dedicating my life to being myself and to rejecting others when they showed themselves to be different. I felt a coward, as if I had never done anything but lie to myself.

In the state of abandonment to which my solitude and my position subjected me, I saw a mountain, a mass, an enormous wave bearing down on me, violently. It was my eighteen years of life. Although I curled up raising one of my knees by way of defence, I could not prevent it from crashing over me. In the absence of all the participants of the world, the world itself also disappeared. Then, the truth appeared to me. I was nobody. It was not an intellectual thought. It was a brutal sensation. All my past personal experiences disappeared, all the acts through which I had shown myself as a person disappeared as well. It was as if I had become lost in unlimited space, with no reference points, as if I had remained suspended in infinity.

Solitary

PART THREE
DESOLATION

> To whom may read it
> [...] Our nothingness differs very little; the circumstance why you are the reader of these exercises and I the writer is ordinary and fortuitous.
>
> Jorge Luis Borges, *Fervor of Buenos Aires*[1]

---

1. *Obras Completas I*, Buenos Aires, Emecé Editores, 1996 [1923], p.16, translated by the author.

Solitary

The corridor on the first floor of the building where I was moved one month before the end of my stay in prison, with four-bed cells on either side. The punishment cell on the fifth floor of the same building opened onto the same kind of corridor, but there were no tables down the middle of it. Only an empty space.

XXVIII

> It was noon, and there was no longer one but Two [...]
> Now we celebrate, united, certain of the victory,
> The feast of the feasts:
> Zarathoustra came, the friend, the host of the hosts!
>
> Friedrich Nietzsche, "From the High of the Mountains"[2]

To say that until then, until my solitary confinement in the punishment cell, I felt complete and considered myself autonomous would amount to saying that I was conscious of it, which does not correspond to the type of consciousness which one normally has of oneself. But I can assert that I had never questioned my feeling of oneness or my autonomy with regards to others. However, without saying that I knew who I was, I can at least imagine that I did not often wonder about it. Doubtless, it was a concept I had incorporated without even realising it. I did not observe who or how I was, I only was. I did not watch myself living, I simply lived. Even though I questioned and criticised the values on which my gender, my family, my social class, my nationality or my origins were based, I did not question the existence of other values which I set against them and for which I fought. As a last resort, the new values I defended strengthened the base of my identity. But my isolation made me realise that I owed everything to others, because, without them, I was nothing.

Nothing is more natural than to believe that all we are is due to ourselves, not only due to what we acquire socially, but also to what nature has given us. We are proud of ourselves as if we had built ourselves, from our name and our body to our values, our ideas, our gender and our nationality. We build our own story, we tell it to ourselves according to what suits us best; we show a certain image of ourselves, we play

---

2. In Hannah Arendt, *The Origins of Totalitarianism*, New York, Harcourt Brace & Company, 1979 [1948].

Solitary

a role. But if those to whom we tell this story disappear, the story disappears as well. We then find ourselves alone with the people to whom, in the framework of our story, we did not attribute any role. We are only accompanied by those we sacrificed, those we put aside because they did not correspond to the image we always wanted to give of ourselves.

Without the presence of those I had shared my story with and who, day after day, gave sense to my life, in the imaginary encounters with others, I felt incapable of defending myself when they attacked me. Not only those who harassed me saw me in a different way, but none of them saw me as I had seen myself until then. Then I lost myself and I did not know who I was any more. The destructive nature of those feelings broke me, made me lose my power and allowed others to act towards me as they wished.

Voluntary withdrawal from daily life provides us with a privileged moment in which to establish dialogue with our own self. Holidays, moments of solitude, retreats, meditation, psychotherapies do good because they allow this dialogue which is a source of energy. In those dialogues, as expressed by Nietzsche in his poem "From the High of the Mountains", *One* can become *Two*, the individuals meet themselves. Sometimes we feel overwhelmed by our daily life, stuck in our narrow restricted monotonous routine, in which case evasion allows us to dream, gives us access to infinity, to a world where everything is feasible, to a world of endless possibilities.

This is what, many years later, when I was already doing my doctorate, Augusto Ponzio, my professor of the Philosophy of Language at the University of Bari, Italy, whose works on the philosopher Emmanuel Levinas I had the luck to read,[3] explained to us. The role we must play all the time, the identity with which we build ourselves throughout our lives, this identity with which we recognise ourselves in front of others, with the rights that it grants us and the duties that it imposes on us, with limited and well-defined responsibility, with all those aspects which are each time more specific as the contractual regulation of our social life becomes more important, requires that we submit ourselves

---

3. *I Segni Tra Globalità e Infinità. Per la Critica della Comunicazione Globale*, Bari, Cacucci Editore, 2003.

to the authority of our *I*, of our identity, of what we imagine society expects of us.

The reduction of our relationships with others to relations based on the position that we occupy in the productive structure and in the social hierarchy, in the field of knowledge and competence, means the negation of our otherness with regards to the identity which we obtain according to this structure. The need for expression of this otherness, this excess with regards to our limited existence, and the urgency which it has to show itself, requires evasion. Our own infinity forces us to meet with ourselves frequently. In that case, it is not only positive for us, but also necessary to take us away from our daily life.

The distancing from the place we occupy in society allows us to become aware of our own relativity. That which took up room in the body leaves a space for the multiple possibilities offered by the universe. At this moment, *one* becomes *two*, the *I* can converse with the *self*. In the dialogue we establish with ourselves during this voluntary evasion, as long as the circle of acquaintances is clear in our minds, and that we feel they are within reach, our *I* remains complete because we know that, when we return to our daily life, we will find it. In this encounter where a dialogue between the *I* and the *self* occurs, our personality, although it may undergo modifications because of positive contact with our otherness, not only remains intact, but is often even reinforced.

In this extract from the first letter I wrote to my family when I arrived in Devoto after the long period of isolation in Córdoba Prison, this encounter with myself is clearly expressed, as well as the positive impact which it had had on me:

> In this type of situation, one tends to cling to the past, which is good because I had a lot of time to analyse quite accurately each one of the things which I lived before. I tried to learn from each of my experiences and I really believe I took enough advantage of all this time I had in which, day after day, one was confronted by oneself. Today I can tell you that I am well, that I am quiet and very impatient to see you to tell you one thousand things.

Solitary

Although being separated from everything and everybody was obviously not a deliberate choice, although this isolation was compulsory, and despite the fact our own lives were permanently threatened, many times in the cell in Córdoba, without being aware of it, I practiced what Nietszche did. Alone with myself, I would close my eyes and revisit my past. It was a positive activity which filled me with hope. I learnt from what I had already experienced, and I imagined an even better future. This constant presence of my dear people in my mind made this exercise possible, even enjoyable.

But if it is always possible for an individual who is alone to establish a creative dialogue with herself or himself, there is also a risk of them falling into a state of solitude. It occurs, the German philosopher Hannah Arendt again says, when, isolated from everybody, their own *self* also abandons them. Then solitude becomes unbearable. Dependent on others to be confirmed in its identity, the *I* can only exist when we live in society, when *I* can address *you*. Otherwise, subjected to solitude, "the man loses confidence in himself as partner of his thoughts and this elementary confidence in the world, necessary for any experience. The *I* and the world, the power to think and the capacity to realise experiences are lost at the same time."[4]

Therefore, if we want to preserve our own identity, it is indispensable that we look at the immediate environment and that we return to the real contact with others. To venture mentally towards new horizons is an exercise of freedom which is positive only if we always keep a link with others. If isolation or solitary life are prolonged, they can easily provoke a situation of solitude which distances us from our reality and make us lose our sense of being. We lose our place in the world; we feel that we are not part of it any longer. As we depend on others to exist, if we stay away from them for too long, we can easily feel that we have disappeared. The contact with people is broken within us. For the French philosopher Cornelius Castoriadis,[5] in the absence of a social environment, the only guarantee of our existence, the radical imagination of our own psyche, finds no obstacle to reproducing the representation of an original state,

---

4. Hannah Arendt, *op. cit.*, p.477.
5. Cornelius Castoriadis, *L'Institution Imaginaire de la Société,* Paris, Éd. du Seuil, 1975, p.439.

previous to the awakening of our awareness as a baby, of being somebody in front of someone else, in this particular case, our mother, the original state in which the *self* is everything and the *I* does not exist.

Solitary

XXIX

[…] part of our existence lies in the feelings of those near to us.
Primo Levi, *If This is a Man*[6]

Because one loses the habit of hoping in Lager,[7] and even of believing in one's own reason. In the Lager it is useless to think, because events happen for the most part in an unforeseeable manner; and it is harmful, because it keeps alive a sensitivity which is a source of pain, and which some providential natural law dullens when suffering passes a certain limit.
Idem, *Ibid*[8]

Every time others recognise us, they confirm who we are. For that reason, when one has been excluded or taken away from the world, if one wants to survive, it is important to keep the mental contact with people who still live in it. In solitary confinement, there was a special moment when the importance of this recognition for our spiritual and moral integrity appeared to me particularly clearly, almost as a revelation. One evening, a few days after I was locked-up, companions from the wing let me know that they loved me very much, and that my mother, my family and my husband also loved me very much. It was as if, being inanimate, they breathed life into me. To convey something apparently so simple, the prisoners installed an ingenious system. Thanks to a set of mirrors one of the prisoners positioned on one side of the toilets, these detected the movements of the guard through a small window to the external corridor. At the same time, two others helped a third to climb up to the window situated at the top of the wall on the other side of the wing. Hanging on to the bars, the prisoner could shout loudly

---
6. *Op. cit.*, p.204.
7. *Lager* is German for "camp"; in Levi's work here "concentration camp".
8. P.203.

towards the opposite block where the punishment cells were. This action was of great value, because of the risk run by the prisoner who did the shouting; they could be discovered and sent to the *chanchos* in their turn.

If by being locked in that cell I had been isolated from the world, these shouts allowed me to make contact with it again. It reminded me, indeed, that the world existed and that within it a place was still reserved for me; my companions in the wing thought of me and kept a space for me. Their shouting caressed me as a warm wave, covering me with its heat. In that absolute solitude, where nothing happened, while nightfall made silence weigh even more heavily on me, the voice of my companions gave me courage and a reason to exist again.

There was also an unexpected event. It was at a moment when nothing gave me the slightest hope. Maybe it was proof that even in situations of the most profound despair, there is always a chance of something we could never imagine. At an unusual time, my cell door was opened and delegates of the International Committee of the Red Cross appeared. Nevertheless, when I wanted to speak to them, I was unable to articulate a single word, and only with great difficulty was I able to stutter some sounds. Galíndez, the director of security at the prison, was next to them. He had taken his usual posture. He was a small man, bald and paunchy, resembling the Italian Fascist dictator Benito Mussolini. He stood arms crossed on his chest, legs spread, his pubis slightly forward, as if the only element he based his authority on was a simple physical attribute. It was he who had made me sign my discharge before locking me up in that cell, and his very presence frightened me, preventing me from speaking.

Seven days had passed before this event. I had had no contact except with the guard, who I was not allowed to speak to. It was only on the eighth day at mid-day that I received the ICRC delegates' visit. We had always considered that such contact took on particular importance. As political prisoners, we all looked forward to receiving visits from representatives of these international humanitarian organizations, and each of us vowed on any such occasions to denounce the bad living conditions inside the prison. But my throat was much too tight. When one of them asked me why I was there and how I felt I could only cry. Between two sobs, I tried to tell the story of the ring.

During her first visit, when we could still touch each other, my sister had given me a small, thin ring. In a certain way, this ring replaced my wedding ring which the military had stolen from me; it was the only object that I had managed to hide for some weeks after the *coup d'état*, wearing it on my finger. When I had been taken to the legal department after my sister's visit in the new visiting room, I denied scratching the table. In front of the delegates, however, I did not dare to repeat this. Seven days of solitary confinement had changed my way of seeing the world and reality. Therefore, I made an effort to tell them what I had invented during the incalculable hours of solitude. To make up for the injustice of my punishment, I had tried to convince myself that, while I had been speaking to my sister, perhaps I had not paid attention to my gestures. I told myself that, without realising what I was doing, I had no doubt let my hand slip and, keeping my fist tightly closed, I had indeed scratched the table with my ring.

But my own tears and the unreality of my story transformed my words into an incoherent and disjointed tale. At that moment, I felt that I had no control over myself; that I could no longer master my actions. My inability to express myself to those men was the first demonstration of my loss of power, my feeling of being nobody in front of others and of my impossibility of refusing what was imposed on me. Still stammering, I limited myself to asking how long I would still be separated from the other prisoners.

The member of the delegation with the foreign accent looked at the head of the security. The latter changed his posture at once and answered: "Fifteen days!" Finally, I was told when my torture would reach its end. But at the same time the idea of having to stay within those four empty walls as many days more as I had done already increased my fear in an exponential way. Nothing lifted this paralysing feeling. If, in the beginning, I had more or less managed to utter just a few sentences, the effect of this information prevented me, definitively, from pronouncing anything further. Words remained stuck in my throat. I then felt guilty for not decrying the miseries to which we were subjected day-after-day, for not explaining to the delegates of the ICRC that the food was of bad quality, that medical care was lacking, that the hours of recreation were insufficient. I felt sick at not doing what I thought my companions in the wing would have expected of me. I felt bad for not saying that twenty-five women lived on top of each other in that wing. But how would I have been able to do so, if all I wished for at that moment was to return to share that situation with them? To return to the wing with my companions, even if the conditions in which they lived were pitiful.

XXX

> When one day the warder told me that I'd been there five months, I believed it but I didn't understand it. For me it was for ever the same day that I was spinning out in my cell and the same task that I was pursuing […] It was the end of the day, the part I don't like talking about, the nameless part, when evening noises would rise up from every floor of the prison in a cortège of silence […] for the first time in several months, I clearly heard the sound of my own voice. I recognised it as the one that had been ringing in my ears for days on end and I realised that all that time I'd been talking to myself. I then remembered what the nurse said at mother's funeral. No, there was no way out and no one can imagine what the evenings in prisons are like.
>
> Albert Camus, *Outsider*[9]

The fortnight expired on Tuesday March 9th at mid-day. But the guard only came to fetch me at ten o'clock at night. When I left that cell, I knew that another prisoner was isolated in a similar cell, just a few steps from the one where I had been. She had been taken to this floor the same day as the delegates of the ICRC had come to see me.

This had been another unexpected turn of events. It was after ten o'clock at night. I knew that because I had already been allowed to bring in the mattress. I was trying to sleep when a chaotic noise invaded the silence of my cell. Yells, knocks, chains and locks opening near me turned the atmosphere into hell. My heart jumped and started beating uncontrollably. Were they coming to take me? This time, were they going to kill me? The doors of the hall opened, steps came towards my cell. But they continued to another cell next to mine. During this time, hanging from the windows, the prisoners of the whole prison struck the bars with jars and metal plates. They shouted that a prisoner had been taken

---

9. Hamish Hamilton, 2000, p.79, translated by Joseph Laredo from *L'Etranger*, 1942.

to the *chanchos*, to the punishment cells, to solitary confinement. They wanted to let the world know what was happening in our prison. They roared desperately that the prisoner had problems seeing, that her punishment would last one month and that, during the isolation, there was a risk that her eyes would deteriorate.

Shortly afterwards, the doors of the wing opened again. This time, the steps came to my cell and the door opened. Although the appearance of a nurse seemed rather strange to me, my fear and my uncertainty quickly disappeared. The Valium that the doctor from the ICRC had prescribed for me that morning did the rest. The result of the visit of those delegates gave the situation a surreal appearance, but that night at least I slept calmly — although artificially. But when seven days later the guard came to fetch me to take me back to the wing, it was very difficult for me to bear the fact that the other prisoner had to live another three weeks through what I had just had to endure. The shouts of the prisoners the night this companion had been punished still resounded violently in my mind, and I feared she would become blind. How could I accept the idea that somebody had to go through what had just crushed me? How could I imagine that anybody could survive this experience whose only recollection destroyed me? How could I help that girl, if… I could not offer her my eyes?

Arriving in the wing, my companions were waiting for me with biscuits and cheese, and the next day they celebrated my return. They showed a particular kindness and tenderness to me. Later, they told me that my sister had sent a telegram informing me that the authorisation for me to leave the country had been refused. They had been able to read it because all the mail which reached us had been opened, read and censored by the prison authorities. This telegram marked the end of the story which had begun with our demonstrations of joy sixteen days earlier, when I had been called to the legal department and we had believed that I would be allowed to leave for France soon. It is true that in the isolation cell I had not thought of release any more, and that the irreversible character of the situation was becoming a part of me; but I was, nevertheless, disappointed by the news. Furthermore, the affection the companions from my wing had shown when shouting through the window now appeared as a kind of consolation for a piece of bad news they already knew. I felt frustrated. But I stopped thinking about that business and I went to the corner of the wing where, hidden from the sight of the guards, we did gym movements, taking turns, before having a shower. It was a way of resuming the routine that I was going to follow in prison for one more long year.

One of our four-bedded cells on the first floor of the new building.

XXXI

> [...] I found myself faced with one of those situations which are the embodiment of nonsense, where some rescue from insanity is necessary but not forthcoming, and where madness yet does not leap into the breach. No doubt I would have gone mad, because it takes a well-nourished brain to cope with such an absolute as Nothing [...]
> Christopher Burney, *Solitary Confinement*[10]

It was difficult for me to write to my family. It took me three days to finish the first letter, which I had begun the day after my return from the punishment cell, on March 10th 1977. In it I told them what I had felt while locked-up, with the only words which I could find at the time:

> The first days, I was very nervous (as I do not remember ever being). I felt a deep powerlessness. When I saw that I was going to be locked up again, totally alone, without the possibility to exchange a word with anyone, I had a sort of crisis of claustrophobia. At certain moments I suffered, and I cried as I felt so defenceless. But nevertheless, I gathered the force, courage and patience I still had left, and I managed to regain self-control and stop worrying.

On an additional sheet, I explained why I had not sent them the letter as soon as I had written it. I told them that I felt quite confused and that I became exhausted quickly.

On March 18th, it was my nineteenth birthday. Towards the end of the day, I received some presents and two beautiful cards from my companions. One of those cards had been drawn especially for that day. The other one was a white sheet folded in two, with a drawing done by the best draftswoman on the wing, the one who had been an architecture

---
10. *Op. cit.*, p.21.

Solitary

student. The drawing showed a girl wiping her tears with a flower-embroidered handkerchief, while she handed a rose to me saying: *This is for you and… we lo… sniff!… ve sniff! you a lot…* and it continued inside the card: *we will miss you.* That card should have been given to me at the moment of my departure abroad. As we were practically sure that that moment was imminent, some prisoners had begun to autograph it. One of them, the companion who asked me the meaning of the words written in French in Tolstoy's novels she used to read, had written:

> The bitter moment of separation has arrived, and although you already know it, I repeat that we shall keep the joy which inhabits you in the palm of our hands, that your smile will make us relive more than a memory, it will make us feel the Gladys who is going away, will stay with us for ever. Just as your taste of freedom continues to fly around our pillows, during the night, our thoughts will turn to your image and to your musical vitality. I wish you, lots, lots of luck. I love you very much.

Another companion wrote to me:

> Sweet and beautiful Gladicín: Who will fill our wing with enjoyment from now onward? But change is movement and it will be for the best. Then, I should console myself by knowing that you are doing well. I hope that you will always keep all your freshness and your tenderness. I love you very much and I am going to miss you enormously. I shall always remember you. Kisses.

But I did not leave. Or rather, yes, I left, but not to the place where we thought I was going. My companions kept the card that they had prepared for me and gave it to me on my birthday, a few days after I came back from solitary confinement. The lady who slept on the bed next to mine had written:

> Gladicín, my little neighbour, we are still together in this world of walls and bars. But time will dictate our separation, and I want to tell you that I shall always keep your sweet pretty face, your simple and impulsive gestures of

tender teenager as well as your serious face in your feminine reasoning in which one guesses the rising maturity. A maturity which accelerates almost unintentionally, almost without being felt, in this irreversible adversity.

Keep your smile and your hope for ever! Remember that the best of maturity is to know how to carry it with grace, humour and simplicity, with gentleness and a lot, a lot of love. I love you very, very much.

I made a real effort to keep that smile and that hope, to get back on my feet again and to continue. In spite of my frequent relapses, I made an effort to be well and to face adverse reality. In April, I had written to my mother:

I'm doing very well, mum. I try to feel better every day. If I have a relapse, I make great efforts to be well. And in the end, I succeed because it's very bad to feel down. There's a saying: "life is like a stair. With the hope we go up, and with the discouragement we go down…".

I send you all the roses of the world and a big, very big hug. One thousand kisses full of love and affection. I love you very much.

But despite the efforts I made to fight the confusion and malaise, it was more and more difficult for me to speak. Until one day I got up with the intention of not doing it any more. We were dealing with the day-to-day problems of running the wing, all of us gathered in the middle of the room, sitting facing each other, on the two rows of beds. I looked around at the oldest companions; it was as if I had wanted to implore them for their protection, as if, by making them notice my silence, I had wanted them to realise that I could no longer cope with imprisonment. That day, I decided that I would not grow up any more. As a way of rejecting the world, my organism, powerless, completely stopped working normally. For years afterwards my body denied life and complained silently, without any language other than pain.

Being obstinate though, in April I wanted to speak to Galíndez, the head of security. I wanted to know if I could get the college books I needed to continue to prepare for the exams that would allow me to finish my college education when I left prison. It was obvious that finishing college represented a fundamental objective in my life. In the first letter I wrote to my family on my arrival at Devoto, having told them that I had thought of them during the isolation in Córdoba, and how I had dreamed about all the beautiful aspects of freedom, I confided in them that:

> When I thought that my classmates were going to graduate soon, a certain sadness invaded me.

Some weeks later, I wrote to my elder sister:

> I feel a profound need to study. I would like to have many books and learn new subjects. I miss studying. My biggest desire is to be able to finish college one day, even though it is by my own means.

When I sent the note to the head of the security, I wrote to my sisters:

> I read an article on genetics in *Clarín* magazine. What a fascinating subject! I always loved these things. And once again, I felt the desire to study. I told myself that now I have the possibility to do what I have wanted to for a long time. Then, very enthusiastically, I drafted a note to the head of security. I think that I could study all the subjects related to the last class. It would be so wonderful! Furthermore, it would keep me busy and would allow me to use my time well. We shall see what happens.

Galíndez let me know that he would have authorised my getting the books if they had been related to studies at a university, but not to college education. Because of the irrationality of the answer, in August I insisted again. This time, Galíndez came to see me personally. The answer was negative, harsh and categorical. The impression he gave of protecting himself behind his grey uniform, and the authority he asserted by rocking in an imperceptible way on his black military boots, gave his refusal a particularly despotic character and increased my anxiety and my stupefaction. He turned his back and left.

I had a lump in my throat. I felt that I was definitively not in my college or in my city any longer, not even in the prison of the latter. The last mental prerogatives with which I had managed to survive until then, as well as project myself beyond this in my imagination, collapsed inside me. The mental spaces I had been able to preserve in spite of all I had undergone continued to disappear. Galíndez' refusal made me become aware that prison was my only reality, and that this apart there was nothing else. After my stay in the punishment cell, his refusal and the authoritarian gesture with which he turned to leave, broke the last links with which I had forced myself to keep in touch with the world. My internal fragility was such that his attitude shook me as if he had hurled a terrible blow. At that moment, it was as if he had slapped me. I had the impression that nobody had previously denied my existence in such a rough and absolute way.

When a young woman is nineteen-years-old, she normally matures and evolves. I was already married and I had even wanted to have a child. As I had written to my mother some time before:

> We do not always see time pass. But sometimes I become aware of the way in which one grows, one evolves and one matures. I realised that I was becoming an adult. Sometimes it saddens me. I have the impression that the years go too fast and that when I am released I will no longer have the chance to do the same things I did before. This thought worries me. Then I think that I can grow, mature, be grown-up; but it does not seem necessary that my spirit has to stop being young, adolescent, spontaneous, full of freshness and enjoyment. Sometimes it is difficult, because the knocks we receive from life … it would seem that they want to force your spirit not to be young any longer. And it does not have to be so, naturally not.

But the reaction of the head of the security caused me to regress and shortly after that I began to call for my mother in my sleep. Galíndez' refusal annihilated me, combined with a profound sense of shame and cowardice. I suffered from not being able to satisfy a personal ambition, my enthusiasm for life, while so many of our companions no longer existed. At that moment, the gesture of that man frustrated my remaining wishes, those which had survived the illusions with which I still managed to project myself into the future with the healthy energy of my own will to exist.

XXXII

> [...] the political sectarianism had penetrated within the wing as an icy needle, and for the first time, I felt a loneliness that could crush me.
> Graciela Lo Prete, *Memories of a Political Prisoner*[11]

The situation in the prison continued to worsen. The terror employed by the repressive forces of the State against the guerrillas at national level had its impact within the prison. The more effective the policy of destroying any opposition became, the stricter were the measures applied to the prisoners' lives. In turn, the attitude of the activists or sympathisers of those groups faced with this new situation was modelled on the attitude taken by their companions outside. They retaliated. They used a policy of confrontation with the authorities. Consequently, the latter progressively restricted our opportunities for action and movement, punished us without mercy, and deprived us of recreation and all kind of contact with the outside.

As for me, my differences with the major groups widened further and created many tensions. The consequences of their policies and attitudes were progressively more difficult to bear. The sanctions increased. The decisions taken by those groups exerted a great influence on the behaviour of all their members and a gap inevitably grew between us. In addition to the differences between us on the day of the first visit of our families in the new visiting rooms, there were many others. The uneasiness between us started in the courtyard on Christmas Day 1976. Although we were not allowed to sing, the members of the major groups decided to do so. They sang partisan songs. The prison authorities handed down a five day long punishment. To be sanctioned in this way meant to be deprived of visits, walks in the courtyard, mail, newspapers, books and any parcel coming from the outside.

---
11. *"La Lopre", op. cit.*, p.152, translated by the author.

I had made no decision about singing, and had not agreed with it. In any case, nobody had consulted me. Yet, though my position within the prison was negligible, I was equally affected by the consequences of their actions. On May 25th 1977, a national holiday, the inmates again sang through the windows. This time it was the national anthem and partisan slogans, which provoked a further penalty of ten days. Over time, I did not even know why we were punished. On Monday, June 13th we received a further punishment until July 2nd and, without that even being over, yet another of seven days, and yet another one which completed the month. In mid-October, there was a new sanction of five days and, a few days later, three consecutive penalties, which meant three more weeks. On November 28th, the authorities condemned us to a new punishment of five days which was extended until December 14th 1977.

Alongside the crackdown, the authorities decided that we would be installed in different wings. That order was consistent with the individual search of each inmate, performed regularly since June 2nd. Until then, the security guards appeared unexpectedly and gave us an order to go out into the courtyard as we were, without touching anything. From that moment onwards, instead, we would be searched individually before leaving the wing, under the pretext that we could hide a suspicious object or incriminating documents. The leaders of the major groups rejected this order and refused to cooperate. Because of this refusal, the prisoners were first shut up in the cells of the fifth floor, then grouped into wings subjected to a stricter regime.

The first time we were searched, nine prisoners from our wing and fifty-seven of the neighbouring wings were taken to the punishment cells. As for the rest of us, we were forced out into the yard. When we returned an hour later, the chaos the guards had caused inside the wing was such that we did not know where to begin to restore order. We had to make our beds and those of our comrades who had been punished, to pick up our stuff and theirs, to prepare the necessary material to be sent to the punishment cells. The wing seemed deserted. We tried to contain our nervousness, but our morale was at its lowest ebb.

However, punishment had some advantages. It allowed members of the same organization not only to have the same experience as their peers but also to be lodged with them in the same wing afterwards. But the stay in the punishment cells was no longer what it was; the prisoners were no longer alone. The refusal to be searched was so great that each cell had to accommodate more prisoners than it could hold. Upon their return, the inmates told anecdotes of what had happened there. The way they laughed and had fun in doing so gave me the impression that in those cells something extraordinary happened that I had personally failed to appreciate while there myself.

Using the search as a selection criterion, the authorities reorganized the structure of the wings and for months they regularly moved prisoners. These movements also accentuated the feeling of being uprooted. It was painful to be split-up from companions with whom we had lived for months. On August 11th of that year, eleven prisoners were permanently moved to another wing and replaced with another ten inmates from the other building. The sadness we felt was overwhelming and we could do nothing but cry.

However, the guards did not search all the inmates. Indeed, the checks were not essential to the selection. I, for example, although I did not intend to refuse, was separated without being searched, and put on the side of the prisoners who would not be punished. The leader of *Montoneros*, who some days before had asked to be transferred to our wing because the conviction of the members in that wing was waning, placed herself between the guard and another inmate who was just about to be searched, in an openly provocative manner. It was obvious that she did not want to go unnoticed and miss the opportunity of refusing to be searched.

After this last search, on December 13th, the authorities took me to a bigger wing, where they regrouped inmates who did not belong to either of the major organizations. At this stage of events, I felt defeated by fatigue, overwhelmed by what was happening, powerless and disappointed by what I saw. The attitude of the prisoner who had provoked the guard in order to get herself punished deeply disappointed me. That day, I wrote the last letter from prison addressed to my mother. I finished it by saying:

Bueno mamita, I assure you I am exhausted by so much accumulated tension. Today, I cannot stand anything anymore.

Although in this new building we did not suffer from so many punishments as before, the rules were even more stringent. New restrictions were imposed, and the smallest details that could make us happy were eliminated. Inside the wing, however, I had a surprise. I was no longer politically isolated in the prison. I was not the only prisoner who did not belong to the major groups and who did not share general ideas. Many of us had experienced similar feelings, and for a long time. This joy roused by my belonging to the group and by sharing my daily life with them was unexpected. I loved the inmates with whom I had been in the previous wing, but the weight of the political atmosphere had begun to seriously exceed the strength of our emotional ties. In this new wing, instead, I did not feel isolated. I could fit in very well and participate in all the conversations and activities. In addition, the physical conditions of this new place were a bit better than those of the wing we had just left.

The building we were now in was the one in which I had been in solitary confinement. But we were on the first floor, not on the fifth. There was a long, wide corridor which left much more space to circulate than the one we had in the wing I had come from. On each side of the corridor there were cells, in each of which four of us slept.

To find myself among women like me, not to suffer any longer from the consequences of sectarianism and discrimination, had a most beneficial effect on my daily life and gave me new confidence. To such an extent that during the visit of one of my sisters, when she expressed her doubts about bringing the clothes I had asked for, I did not hesitate for a second to tell her in a light tone that she should present the clothes at the entrance where she was searched, specifying the wing I was in. My comment must have sounded as if it was implicit support for the differential system recently introduced in the prison, and the "privileges" we enjoyed in relation to the inmates located in the wings governed by stricter rules. My sister reacted angrily. Using the authority of her age, she scolded me and told me that she absolutely refused to play into the hands of the prison authorities. I was sorry she could not understand what it was like to constantly suffer the consequences of the provocative policy pursued by the major opposition groups and, thus, a gap opened up between us. I felt humiliated by such an unflattering image and the lack of any spirit of dignity and integrity. With this new fracture in my emotional support, my inner loneliness continued to deepen.

Solitary

XXXIII

> [...] that day I also experienced that very same tenseness, that same itchy feeling and clumsiness that came over me when I was with them, that I had occasionally felt at home: as if I weren't entirely okay, as if I didn't entirely conform to the ideal; in other words, somehow as if I were Jewish. That was a rather strange feeling, because, after all, I was among Jews and in a concentration camp.
>
> Imre Kertész, *Fatelessness*[12]

My journey through the various prisons ended shortly afterwards. Ten months had passed since I had been confined in the isolation cell. In Christmas week 1977, we asked the authorities to bring us the newspaper on the 24th. Indeed, we no longer received newspapers daily, as had been the case before our transfer to that last wing, but only three or four times a week. And on November 25th we had read that at Christmas, numerous prisoners would receive permission to leave the country. We also hoped that a list would be published with the names of the prisoners concerned. In 1978, Argentina would host the World Cup football tournament and to do so the military would have to demonstrate that it satisfied certain requirements of democracy and respect for human rights as upheld by the international community. Although prisoners had been released throughout the year, we thought that this time we would read the longest list of prisoners released since the military *coup d'état* around two years before.

When we heard the shout of the guard announcing that the newspaper had arrived, we rushed to the companion who had managed to grab it. We pressed around her as she began to read names aloud, having spread the newspaper on the big granite table in the middle of the gallery. Not able to wait until my name was quoted — this time I was sure it would

---

12. Evanston, Illinois, USA, 1992, p.102, translated by Christopher C Wilson and Katharina M Wilson from *Sorstalanság*, 1975.

be there—I climbed on a bench so as to read over all the heads. I knew where to look for my name. My eyes scanned the list from top to bottom in a flash and stopped at the names of the prisoners authorised to leave the country. At once, I found mine. It was there! I also saw the names of one of my two cousins held in the same prison as me. It was a moment of profound emotion.

This permission to leave the country was the response to the third request presented by my family to the NEP. After each negative answer, we had to wait three months to ask again and the decision, in turn, took three supplementary months. If this was unsuccessful, we had a right of appeal, which took three more months to be dealt with. In that way, more than nine months passed since the refusal of the second request, the one that I had learnt about by reading the telegram sent by my sister on my return from solitary confinement. It was thanks to the ceaseless action of my mother and my sisters in Argentina, my husband in France, international organizations such as the United Nations High Commission for Refugees, French bodies, such as *France Terre d'Asile* (the French solidarity movement) or even the President of the French Republic, Valéry Giscard d'Estaing, who had signed a letter addressed to the Argentinean Government demanding my liberation, that I had finally been able to obtain authorisation to leave the country.

In addition to the absence of physical contact between the two different sectors of prisoners inside the prison, which meant two different regimes, the sad state of our relations could be detected when a prisoner was occasionally released, or when somebody left the prison for any other reason. When it was a mate from their part of the prison, the joy, the farewell shouts, the words of affection, the promises of eternal memory and the wish for a free life, full of love and friendship, came from all the windows, including in our sector. That did not happen when the prisoner was leaving from our own sector. The morning when the policemen came to fetch me to take me to the airport, only voices from within our wing were heard. In the other buildings, the silence was almost total.

As I left the prison, my companions in captivity did not cheer me. The two or three voices I distinguished, in an isolated way, made the silence more eloquent in that prison full of political prisoners. Among those there were many who, while I was in solitary confinement, had let me know that they loved me. There were also those with whom I had shared the long months of isolation during the military occupation in Córdoba. As a consequence of not refusing orders, power had intervened and separated us. With us or against us. Power against power. It was no longer a question of fighting for the expression of all, but for the hegemony of power. From now on, I was part of the others, of those who could not be transformed into equals, of those who must be rejected.

In Córdoba, before the *coup d'état*, every time a companion left the prison, we sang the *Bella Ciao*[13] loudly: *Una mattina mi son svegliato, O bella ciao, bella ciao, bella ciao ciao ciao, Una matiiinaaaa, mi son svegliato, E ho trovato l'invasooooore*. We forced our voices, altogether, to sing *ciao* three times. We passed on all our fervour by singing *E se io muoio da partigiano, O bella ciao, bella ciao, bella ciao ciao ciao, E se io muoiooo da partigianooo, Tu mi devi seppelliiir*. With pomp and bravery, we finished the song by saying that the partisan would be *Morto per la libertàààà*. Dead for freedommmm! Tears wet my eyes; the words of the song and the effect of the choir moved me deeply. I imagined the day when my companions would sing it for me and I held on to my illusion.

That morning in Devoto, instead, when I left my cell for the last time, the silence from the other sectors of the penitentiary transformed my walk as far as the gate into a distressing and intimidating one. In spite of the absence of any human being other than the guard, who followed me along this enormous corridor, I felt as if dozens of people were pointing at me. As so many other times in my life, I felt inadequate. But now it was even stranger, to walk alone, in silence, near to so many left-wing activists, in a prison that was part of the social system which we had all tried to change.

If during solitary confinement, my identity had been broken, by leaving the prison, the ignorance of my companions prevented me from existing. After so much shared life and death, their gesture reflected void and nothingness, their silence enveloped and crushed me. Having been *we*, they transformed me into the *other*, into scrap, into something

---

13. Song of the Italian partisans.

which had no right to exist. I was ashamed to leave the prison. So long anticipated, so often imagined and idealised, my freedom only meant a simple change of place.

PART FOUR
MY RELEASE, EXILE…

> If what remains from the experience of torture can ever be something more than an impression of nightmare, then it is an immense astonishment, and it is also the feeling of having become a stranger to the world, a deep state that no kind of ulterior communication with people will ever compensate.
>
> Jean Améry, *Beyond Crime and Punishment*[1]

---

1. *Op.cit.*, p.94.

Solitary

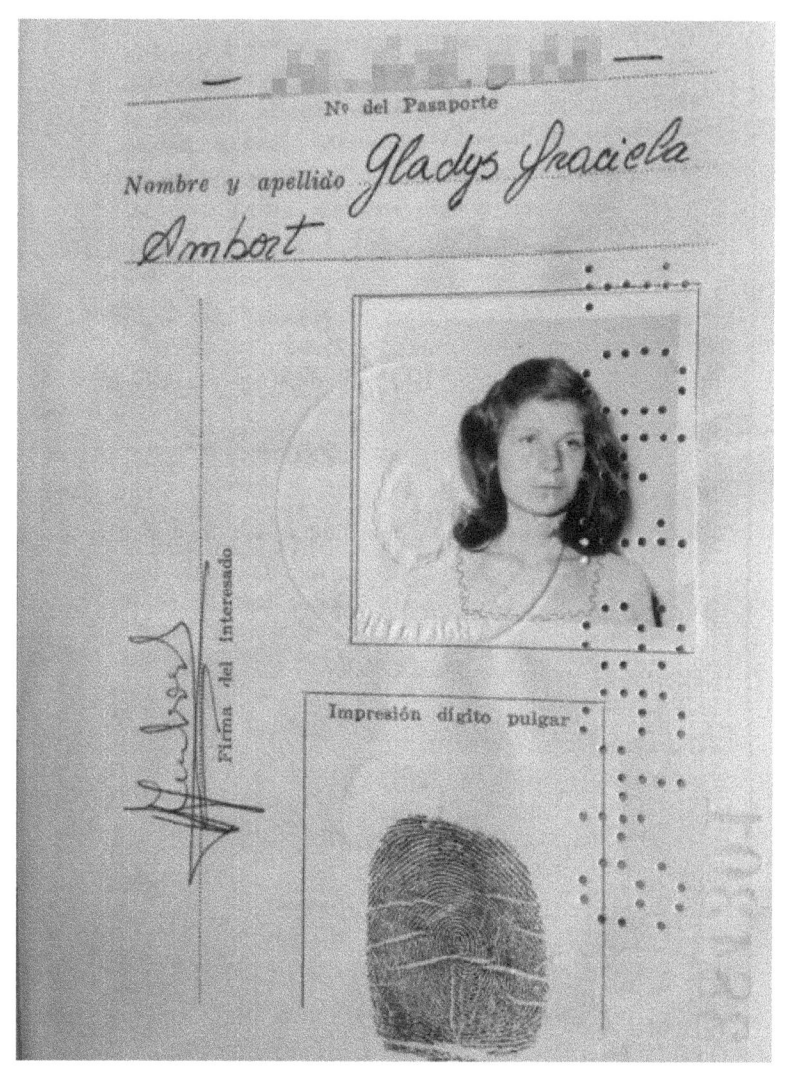

My Argentinean passport aged nineteen. The picture was taken in prison a few days before being taken to the airport.

XXXIV

> [...] we have learnt that our personality is fragile, that it is much more in danger than our life; and the old wise ones, instead of warning us "remember you must die", would have done much better to remind us of this greater danger that threatens us.
>
> Primo Levi, *If This is a Man*[2]

My journey to France was the last step in finally losing everything which had made me somebody: my family, my college, my friends, my city, my country, my language, my past; even the prison I had lost, the prison which initially I had shared with others. At Charles de Gaulle Airport, recently built, ultramodern and sparkling, my husband, who I no longer believed in, was waiting at the end of a conveyer belt. I had the impression he was a stranger to me; however, I closed my eyes and I told myself: "This is my only reality". He was a man I no longer recognised, but my status as a married woman obliged me to accept.

France had granted me political asylum and the United Nations High Commissioner for Refugees had paid for my plane ticket. In France I was warmly welcomed. Most people showed a deep sense of solidarity and treated me with sincere friendship, which I shall never forget. But the loneliness, fear and uncertainty I harboured inside me could find no refuge. The endless administrative steps I had to take on the freezing mornings of a French winter to keep my status as a political refugee reignited the intense pain of exile. The forms I had to complete seemed to symbolise this lack of identity. Indeed, the social security code attributed to foreigners was the figure 99. My innards rebelled constantly. They seemed to confirm the resemblance between 99 and NN,[3] that is all those who do not belong to anywhere and who cannot be identified.

---

2. *Op. cit.*, p.57.
3. In Latin, *nomen nescio*, literally, "I do not know the name". The inscription NN is usually placed on the graves of unidentified bodies (as with Jane or John Doe in some English-speaking countries).

Solitary

At the press conference organized by the CIMADE in February 1978, some weeks after my arrival in Paris, sitting next to Simone de Beauvoir and the group of lawyers who fought for human rights, I gave details about my stays in various prisons in Argentina, I spoke to the listeners, but I could not shorten the distance which separated us. It was a distance which would grow with time, which had begun when I left the cell where I had been locked-up for fifteen and a half days, which had been worsened with my isolation inside the prison and which would deeply influence the route I would follow later.

In a letter I sent to my two sisters from the prison, after the long period of isolation in Córdoba, I had written:

> I assure you that everything was very long, too hard and painful. We had to go through many things which are not easy to imagine [...] Not being able to do anything, days were long, and the solitude of my cell was favourable to thinking over and over again. The last period, I thought too much about freedom; I missed my dear people and well, you see, all those things that the word freedom means and that I saw so limited in a cell of three meters by one [...] I would wish so much to look at somebody tenderly, to give affection, to have an affable and friendly conversation; I would like to feel the maternal tenderness, the love of my husband, I would like to be embraced by my brothers and sisters. I look forward to doing what I had no occasion to do for a long time. I would like to run in the countryside, to cycle, to study, to have a child, to experience everything that can be done daily.

Now that I had finally left the prison, instead, I felt empty, with no self-image, without substance, as if I was dead inside. How to become human again after returning from a world where everything was designed so that one was no more, when the feeling of being somebody and being able to have any desire at all was taken away?

On January 19th 1977, one year before travelling to France, shortly after I signed a request to go into exile and one month before being placed in solitary confinement, this is what I had written to my mother:

My Release, Exile…

> When I think about the trip abroad, I feel sad; in regard to my feelings, it's difficult for me to accept all what going away means, to part from the family and from so, so many things I've got here. When I signed the request to leave the country […], I was a little bit sad. I thought that I would leave my family and the people I love, that I would not see the places which are so dear to me again, that I would no longer go up the stairs which lead to our home, and it hurt me. I had difficulties in accepting that I would not finish college; as well as I would not carry out projects with which I toyed with for so long, since my childhood perhaps. All this saddened me, hurt me. To be forced to abandon the country in which I lived all my life is very difficult. But nevertheless, I often think of what my life in a distant country can be, and I am not afraid.

But when I arrived in Paris, I was not only a foreigner in another country, I felt a foreigner in society and in the world in general. In the mental space kept for my dear people, my roots, my projects, powerlessness and fear, nonsense and insecurity had taken root. Despite being reunited with the world and with all my people, I felt alone and, in fact, when effectively I was alone, I could not keep their memory in my mental sphere. During the following years in Paris, I suffered from not being able to be what I had wished to be in life, but especially not being able to explain why. If in the past I had found it normal to go to school, to want to get married and have children, to choose a profession or militate, after my prison experience, I did not know who I was anymore; I could not identify with anything or anybody. I felt that I did not fit into any social system at all.

The military had not shot me, they had not thrown my body from a plane into the sea. As one extreme left activist from Argentina in Geneva asked me many years later, what did I have to complain about? To understand solitude, the experience of being abandoned by everything and by everyone, the philosophers suggest we keep in mind that one day we will leave this world, which will continue as before and for the continuity of which we will be superfluous. It would seem that nothing is worse than death, but we rarely think of the fragility to which the intrinsic dependence of our person with regard to others condemns us as long as we live.

Solitary

Even today, it seems to me that I shall never be able to explain what I lived through or my sensations in their totality, that I shall always carry it in me without being able to clearly transmit it. Similar to dreams, what I manage to glimpse leaves always a part in the shadows, because all what happened in prison cannot be totally understood by our sphere of thought and by our perception of reality; it escapes the domain of ideas and reality; it escapes any conceptualisation and cannot be explained. In terms of psychoanalysis, according to the Belgian Paul Verhaeghe,[4] the difficulty of passing on what one lived consists above all in the impossibility of giving a representation of what one felt.

But if the trauma brought about by the break is difficult to interpret, the traces it left and the forms in which it showed itself when I resumed contact with people and the world can be easier to understand. As Primo Levi expresses in the profoundly beautiful and sensitive testimony that he left about his dramatic experience in a concentration camp in Poland during the Nazi occupation, all our relations, our affects and our daily habits, and even the smallest objects each of us possesses, hold meaning and are filled with experiences and with memory, so that those who lose them become lost themselves.[5] This is what I felt: something had broken inside of me, I did not possess myself any more, and in spite of having met others and the world again, I was nobody, and I did not belong to this world any more.

If in the past I did not perceive situations from the established social codes, when I left prison I could not do it from those from which, we, the left activists, had wanted to replace those codes. From those positions, which one finds on one side or on the other, it is always easy to judge. For me they had disappeared. Beyond the conventional social vision which governs the majority of our societies and which imposes itself constantly, beyond even the vision which criticised it and tried to replace it, I began to float in doubt and uncertainty, devoid of any order of ideas which would inspire security. My mental confusion was great; in contrast to those who embrace a dogma, or those who are always so

---

4. *L'Amour Aux Temps de Solitude. Trois Essais sur le Désir et la Pulsion*, Paris, Éd. Denoël, 2000, p.234.
5. Primo Levi, *op. cit.*, p.31.

My Release, Exile …

sure of themselves, or those who cannot accept that one can think outside of received schemas, either cultural, religious or political, I never knew what I should think.

I had difficulty in facing the people around me, particularly when I felt that they wanted to impose their views, or simply to exclude everything which, in their determinist logic, could not exist. I also felt particularly bad in front of those who, claiming a so-called heroic spirit, condemned me for being unable to assimilate what I had had to experience, for feeling powerless faced with what had happened to me; in fact, for allowing myself to suffer.

After two years of bearing so many extreme trials, which had been difficult to assimilate, solitary confinement profoundly damaged my personality; the structure which had maintained it up until then collapsed. But the *I* being broken does not mean its definitive disappearance. As long as one continues to perceive the outside world, one has the possibility of recovery. It is the fracture which provokes the pain. It is the fact of feeling others' power in every faultline, in every crack of the *self*.

On my return from nothingness, where there are neither models nor references, where the *I* does not exist and where there is no authority, I felt strongly what power is and I became aware of its omnipotence. I began to understand power from the moment I lost mine. With a pierced and battered *self*, I was disarmed and I felt too exposed to the power of others. The habit people have of imposing or repressing hurt me. It gradually became an obsession. Faced with these attitudes, not only did I feel shrunken, but it was impossible not to mentally project them towards more complex situations, taking on more seriousness. Inside me they acquired the proportions which they would have reached had we not been protected by laws, by contracts and social norms, written or not. The violence of people's reaction when an assertion displeased them, or simply when something did not suit them, appeared to me in an almost tangible way. The resulting power which they exercised daily in their relations with others was like an open sore, like a scratch across the breast. I had become very vulnerable. Finding no models of identification which suited me, not being able to say who I was any more, I was blocked by the power of others. When it was strong, even though it was not deliberate, I was so anxious that I felt as though I would disappear. I had lost all references and all parameters; my internal solitude was total.

It was only when I took refuge in the recollection of that isolation cell where I had been locked-up that I felt protected from people and the world. My only defence was to tell them silently what happens when one is left alone, locked-up, when in the meeting with oneself the self breaks and one loses all one's power. My thought in their respect was always the same: if it happened that they were isolated some day, with a complete inability to act, and without anybody to call upon, they would realise that all the values on which their personality and their social role are built are not values in themselves, but only instrumental, incidental, short-lived and superficial values which disappear as soon as the people around them, who confirm them in this role, disappear as well.

If it were to happen to them, they would lose the power to feel better or superior to others, any guarantee of being and any assurance to assert whatever, any right to possess, and any sense of autonomy and freedom. If one day they remained alone, cut off from others, they would realise that without others, their power exists no more.

XXXV

> [...] a man is a man, and the little reasoning power he may possess is of small advantage, or of none at all, when passion rages and he is oppressed by the limits of humanity.
> Wolfgang Goethe, *The Sorrows of Young Werther*[6]

On the practical and social levels, I had to learn to live again. From the point of view of ideas, I could no longer accept any ready made answers. I had to question everything and work it out again. In order to cling to life, I decided to resume college, take up my secondary education which the gravediggers of life, the denigrators of diversity in my country, had prevented me from finishing. With this idea in mind, one-and-a-half years after leaving prison, and just after my divorce, I went to a college on the outskirts of Paris. As I arrived at break time, I noticed the noise that the pupils made in the courtyard and realised that I was not seventeen anymore. However, I was not twenty-one either. I was ageless.

The idea of finding young people capable of laughing and playing was unbearable to me. Consequently, I never finished my college education. This would prevent me from taking up a career of my choice. So, I headed towards other domains of studies which I had never considered before. In Paris I was able to study Social Sciences without having a college diploma. I imagined that by doing so, I would manage to understand. But in the academic environment, in spite of the application with which I worked at subjects as varied as Sociology, Economics, History or Psychology, I was not attracted by any of them in particular. Inside each one of them I met power again, and none of them allowed me to understand what I wanted to know.

---

6. *Op. cit.*, p.49.

Solitary

I had difficulty in making the daily choices we are permanently forced to make, and besides, I was not able to recognise any value in my "aims" once I had reached them. In none of them did I find what I was looking for, even if I did not know what that was. Identification, the feeling of belonging, of social advancement, of personal development and competence that every individual looks for through instruction and training, barely satisfied my aspirations. Besides, my prison experience and what I had learnt in prison was neither useful nor productive anywhere.

Fortunately, literature threw me a lifeline, a sheet anchor in the middle of the sea. The constant return to books gave me a reason to exist. In books, I often found what I had lived. I felt this great sensation of liberation and assurance which comes from the experience of sharing the same point of view or a feeling. The writers also wrote about what I did not know how to explain. The young Werther, whose story is told by Goethe, was capable of establishing physical limits to human suffering, and of pointing out the uselessness of reasoning to avoid it. Writers such as the Italian Alberto Moravia showed that literature makes it possible to express a feeling or a sensation in a place and exactly the opposite three pages later. It allowed a reconciliation with oneself and with one's own difficulty in making judgments.

Apart from the pleasure of the aesthetic dimension of literature, I appreciated the possibility of changing from reality frequently. When I opened a book, I had the impression of penetrating into a new, mysterious and unexplored universe. In the course of its pages, I found the means to formulate what in life I did not always manage to express; what I could not make people accept; what was forbidden, censored, much of it rejected by the people around me (even before I tried to express it); all that one should not think.

Literature put me in touch with an infinite number of possible worlds, at the same time opening the doors to my own otherness, making it live, letting it express itself. Literature allowed me to recognise the otherness in me, and through it, others. Literature offered me the possibility of restoring the unity necessary for existence. The otherness represented by literature allowed me, while reading it, to find an identity.

By reading I was able to keep alive the values and principles for which I had militated and to consider, with even more lucidity than before, the state of alienation in which we live in our society; we have no grasp of our reality, we do not control what we do; we do not possess what we produce; we believe that if we do not consume, life is not really life. However, when I was young, I believed that getting rid of the bad people was enough for the good ones to be able to build a better society, devoid of misery and suffering. My experience in prison made me think that the new ideas I had embraced to resist those that constituted the base of the society in which I lived, were no kind of guarantee of improving the prosperity of all; they were only to the advantage of those who thought likewise. We only replaced one value by another, one would-be absolute truth by another. In my isolation cell, nevertheless, there was no replacement, the breach was radical. Then, the relativity of truth appeared to me in a visceral way; I realised that we were not fighting to have our truth as another relative truth, as a different truth, but for the imposition of a truth which, as just as it seemed to us, was no less absolute. Now, faced with an absolute truth, the existence of any other truth is unacceptable.

Furthermore, we thought of power originating in high political spheres and being exercised over all sections of society. We believed that we only needed to take that power and fight the enemy to obtain the emancipation of all humanity. Besides, we believed that history was governed by objective and true laws, independent of the society which builds it, unchained from the people who make that history. Instead of promoting the reunion of society with itself, instead of fighting for its autonomy, we thought that there was a single truth and a single road to achieving it; it was then necessary to eliminate all those who prevented us from moving along this road to impose the theory with which we identified.

A few days after the end of my solitary confinement, while I was walking in the yard, I met one of the political leaders from the People's Revolutionary Army. She came from the same prison as I did, in Córdoba. Suddenly I had a recollection of the visits of my mother and my sisters in that prison, and I remembered that this woman had questioned me insistently about them. Who they were, what they did, how they thought, what their political ideas were. Very young, I had rejected my Catholic education based on a so-called truth which involved the worship of a personified divinity; but, that day, I realised that if the extreme left-wing organizations had managed to take power in the name of another so-called truth, my mother and many of my dear ones would have been at least persecuted. It was also from my experiences in prison that I became aware of the aberration of defending a political system which, to impose itself, considers it indispensable, necessary or justifiable to eliminate part of its population, even one of its members.

Contrary to the ideas which circulated among the young people who wanted to found a better society, when I left prison I had from then on two suspicions: that power greatly exceeds the dichotomy between the oppressor and the oppressed; and that the economic dimension is a by-product of power and not the opposite. Of certainties, I only had one: no truth, whatever it is, justifies the elimination of those who oppose it: a human being is an end in itself; nothing can justify her or his alienation, torture or sacrifice.

XXXVI

> Rebuilding things with your mind, avoiding the snares of memory.
> After so many years, I no longer feared my distant—very
> distant—past. It now belonged to a stranger. When I remembered, I was not afraid of dying of nostalgia anymore. I did not
> even need to burn or rearrange any images. I had grown stronger
> than the temptation of tears that led toward a different tunnel. I
> looked at my memories as if they belonged to someone else.
>
> Tahar Ben Jelloun, *This Blinding Absence of Light* [7]

> If I lost my life, my time […]
> If I lost my voice […]
> If I was thirsty, if I was hungry, if I lost everything
> Which was mine and which turned out to be nothing,
> […] I can still speak.
>
> Blas de Otero, *At the Beginning*

In the documentary produced fifteen years later for the International Committee of the Red Cross by Christine Ferrier, and directed by Joëlle Comé, I spoke about what a lawyer from Lyon, France had told me some time before. It was the result of research carried out by a group working under her direction: they did not torture us to make us speak, they tortured us to keep us silent, to prevent us from speaking ever again.

Since my departure into exile, I have travelled a particularly long and, to say the least, not very conventional road. In fact, the different studies I was always stubbornly determined to pursue had a fundamental purpose: to retrieve my ability to speak, the thing that allows us to be,

---

7. Tahar Ben Jelloun, *op. cit.*, p.113.

to feel that we exist and to say who we are. When one lives in the midst of barbarity, it is difficult to distinguish it, it seems normal, it is part of our daily life, and we let it settle on our body even though it hurts. We need it in order to escape the nothingness and to protect our identity from a total breakdown. Throughout the thirty years that passed before I completed the first version of this book in Spanish in 2007, I tried to distance myself from the barbarity that dominated us, and to consider the possibility that it is not necessary to live with it inside me to know who I am. Laboriously, I have woven a new skin which can hold me and protect me. Thanks to this process, I have managed to create a new life; with the birth of my son, everything around me lit up and took on a new sense.

The wound made by the forced interruption of my education, however, has never stopped re-opening. I even think of it at present… It is true, I say to myself, with regret, that I obtained several university degrees, and that I even managed to obtain a doctorate in Humanities. But I was never able to finish my college education, which, like all young people in the world, I should have continued with, in order to follow my chosen career. Furthermore, I am only able to write in block letters, and rather slowly. I had indeed to modify my way of writing when my family informed me that an employee of the mail office in Devoto Prison had pointed out on one of my first letters: "Next time/clearer writing or it does not pass/warn the inmate".

However, now that I have reached the summit of my life, I can survey this road travelled with a quieter and calmer eye. It is true that I did not finish college, but I have been able to face all the obstacles which I found on the way up. And thanks to that, I have got rid of much weight which overburdened me and hurt me. On the way down, I feel lighter…

༄

As for Pablo, my schoolmate whose memory had overwhelmed me during solitary confinement, I knew that he had been denounced by Tránsito Rigatuso, Director of the Manuel Belgrano College of Commerce, who had given the Army a list of pupils and alumni who were to be eliminated. Apparently, my name also appeared on that list, although I had left that college one year earlier. Indeed, when I saw my sister in Devoto Prison, after almost nine months of isolation in Córdoba Prison, she told me that, during that period, the paramilitary continued to look for me on the outside.

One day in May 1976, at eleven o'clock at night, members of their bands, badly-informed, had entered my family home, where I had lived until I got married, almost a year earlier. They arrived in one of those dark Ford Falcons with which they terrorised the population. They entered violently, machine-guns in their hands, and asked to see me. They ill-treated and intimidated my mother and my brother, they stole a kitchen knife, tore out the WC pan and went away. This raid on my family house coincided with the date on which numerous students and ex-students of our school disappeared. My sister, who is a journalist, pointed out in her research work about the young people of the Manuel Belgrano College after the fall of the military junta, that the law courts confirmed this version.[8] All the names were on a list the director of the college had supplied to the extreme right-wing groups attached to the Army, responsible for murders and disappearances in the city. This is how I know that Pablo was among those murdered during the military dictatorship.

What I did not know, was that Pablo was shot on January 29th 1977, in La Plata, in the province of Buenos Aires, and that his body may have been kept at the morgue of that same city until February 5th. It was on the 21st of that month that I was locked-up in the punishment cell where his image penetrated my spirit. Or did I dream it?

Pablo was born on May 25th 1957. When the military killed him, he was nineteen-years-old... *nineteen-years-old, a child's face*... In Argentina, at the time, it did not draw too much attention.

---

8. Mónica Ambort, *"Los Chicos del Belgrano. Del Centro de Estudiantes al Campo de Concentración"*, in *Córdoba. Historias de Amor, de Locura, de Muerte*, Córdoba, Opolop Ediciones, 2000.

Solitary

EPILOGUE

Never Again

At the time of publication of this English edition, over forty years have passed since that press conference in February 1978, some weeks after my arrival in exile in Paris, where what I said failed to translate what I really felt and where the journalists saw *a child's face*.

A child's face? Did they not realise that I was only a spectre? My soul had left with the others. The others? They, those whose mothers still speak out. They lost their children. They speak about them, they have become mad. This is what the soldier called them, he did not know how right he was![1] They are madwomen. They are mad with pain, mad with despair. They raise their children's pictures around Government House. They all look so young, they all look so beautiful. Such young faces, such beautiful eyes.

We wanted to dream, we wanted to fly. Our youth was all energy, all fervour, the new world was there at hand. Diversity was excluded, differences excluded. We wanted to change our society in which too many children did not eat enough, many of them died, others were cold and there were so many others who could not learn how to write the word "Mum". Modernity pushes the elderly aside and freedom exists only in the Economics books of the Americans. We wanted to change society, but they eliminated us all.

---

1. In 1978, during the World Cup, when a journalist from the French newspaper *Le Monde* asked a soldier who those women were who were parading around the obelisk in Plaza de Mayo, asking the junta for their missing children, the latter replied, "Do not pay attention to them, they are Mad."

Physical death, kidnapping, detention, torture, exile, they killed us all. We carry our dead fellows in us, not to leave anybody behind...[2]

Her name was Isabel, her skin was smooth as velvet. It was she who taught me how to massage your temples, something you love so much.

Diana! She was cheerful. She did not want to eat olives, she wanted to keep her fine waist. She had beautiful hair, Diana. They tore it out. After that, nothing more... She was beautiful, Diana, she was cheerful.

Marta. How could I not remember her? She taught me how to sing. Beautiful children songs. We did not always defend the same truth. We did not necessarily share the same values. However, she should have stayed with us. But no. She had her baby, girl or boy? Nobody remembers; they took her far away, there, from where nobody returns.

Him, all I knew about him was that he was a doctor. I thought that he was already forty-years-old. It was a lot compared to my eighteen years of life. But he was actually only twenty-six. In this yard covered with granite and lime, on this sterile ground on which they had fastened and tortured him, there, in the place where the coldness took his heart, a white iris grew as though it wanted to speak of him.

Paco was a young dad; his wife, near us, had just offered him a child. He was breathless all at once, he threw himself on the ground; the lieutenant asked him to say his last prayers. I do not know if this is what he really wanted; to stay alive, I am sure he did. It was not the asthma which took his life, but the pistol of a criminal soldier. Or was it just the pistol of an unmindful soldier? Paco was a young dad. His baby came to life in prison, right by the place where he was killed soon afterwards.

---

2. "*Y así seguimos andando/Curtidos de soledad/Y en nosotros nuestros muertos/Pa' que nadie quede atrás*", extract from the song *Los Hermanos* by Atahualpa Yupanqui, often performed by Mercedes Sosa. "And so we still walk/Tanned by loneliness/And we take our dead fellows with us/Not to leave anybody behind", translated by the author.

Víctor Hugo, where is he? He, my friend, my lover. You picked the first flowers from my garden, you were not anymore. What a horror! What a despair! Why so much hatred? Why so many crimes? Why did they instil so much terror?

Elías, my old Elías, my lawyer, what did they do to him? He who defended me, why did they destroy him like this?

Them, all of them, they were so many, they were all so handsome. Their portraits are still reflected in the crystals formed by each one of our tears. Their names resound as an echo in our memories and ask us not to forget them.

❧

A child's face? Nineteen-years-old? Didn't they realise that I was not any age any more? I had exceeded all the ages. I was beyond. There, where life has not the same sense any more. In my world, melancholy and sadness mix and take me away from humanity, submerge me in my solitude, in my lack of reason, in my nonsense.

María Rosa, she was so young and her womb already sheltered a child. Child of a clandestine dad…I remember. She was hardly nineteen-years-old. *Nineteen-years-old, a child's face…* Only two years older than me. At this time, prison did not conjugate in dead tenses. We were young, we were beautiful, our prison mates had chosen us to be queens. Later, she was a mother and until now I remember her. She had a round womb when she left and three days later she came back; she was not alone any more, her baby occupied each one of her moments. The soldiers, did they at least take her handcuffs off while she offered the fruit of her hope to the world? She was able to keep her baby an additional day, not one more. I still hear her shrieks. I will always hear them. She was nineteen-years-old, they came to take her child. I still see her, I shall never forget. If someone had torn an arm from her, it would certainly have hurt her less. He was big, he was awkward the soldier. Did he understand what he was doing? She agreed to give him her baby, she immediately took it back. The girls helped her, they kissed her, they consoled her, nothing was enough. Nineteen years later, her screaming accompanied me while I had my own child. And while my bosom full of milk made me discover a new pain, I thought of her, with her breasts burning and her little one taken away.

With Marta, my cousin, we pretended nothing had happened in the meantime. Did they understand what had happened to us? No, I do not think so. But I did not speak. Everything had happened so long before. We have seen each other since, more than once. That had been in New York. Her womb bled, mine roared. In the prison hospital, it was already like that. Exile had lasted for so long, maybe she thought that I had forgotten her. I did not speak. She spoke about her boyfriend...his crushed skull. She laughed, I was unable to say a word. Although I did not understand my silence, I understood her laughter, I understood her horror. Is it easier to understand the tragedy of others than one's own pain? Her womb bled, mine roared. In prison, when we were adolescents, it was already like that. My cousin with sparkling eyes, with mischievous glance, I did not speak, it hurt too much.

FORTY YEARS LATER…

In February 2017, I was thunderstruck by what I read in an article about an event I had never heard mentioned before. Forty years earlier, the president of the military junta, General Jorge Rafael Videla, accountable for the torture and killing of thousands of activists and political opponents, and for the theft of babies born in captivity, who died in prison in 2013 after taking full responsibility for his actions but without ever regretting them, had been the target of an attack.[3]

On Friday, February 18th 1977, three days before that fatidic Monday when the head of security decided to punish me and put me in solitary confinement, three members of the People's Revolutionary Army had tried to assassinate General Videla. The action, called *Operación Gaviota* ("Operation Seagull"), was the final attempt to eliminate the tyrant. The plane which was taking him, his Minister of the Economy, José Martínez de Hoz and other members of the high command of the Argentinean Army to an official meeting in Bahía Blanca, was supposed to be blown-up by two bombs before it took off. The operation failed. When the first device exploded, the plane had just taken off. It was already fifteen metres in the air. The second and most powerful one never went off. The scene of the unsuccessful attack was Jorge Newbery Airport, fifteen kilometres from our prison in Villa Devoto. Had the attack succeeded, how many political prisoners might it have cost? Could I have written this story? We were their main hostages. Every time the military suffered an attack by the guerrillas, be it successful or not, they retaliated with punishment measures within the prisons. Such was the case of the plan I have mentioned earlier in this book conceived by the military in the penitentiary at Córdoba, where they, the soldiers themselves, were digging a tunnel to create the appearance of an escape attempt by political prisoners so as to have an excuse to execute us. This time, after this

---

3. Mario Santucho, *"Matar al Tirano"*, in *Revista Crisis*, February 2nd 2017: http://www.revistacrisis.com.ar/notas/matar-al-tirano.

crucial attack, one might suppose that inaugurating punishment cells that particular Monday was at least part of their retaliation. Only five prisoners accepted to go to the new visiting room, and they chose me, one of the five. They must also have taken the refusal of the majority of the prisoners to receive visits from their relatives as justification to deprive them of their daily hour in the yard for a week or so, or having any news from outside, either through the newspapers or the post.

May this frustrated tyrannicide have been the real reason for my being put in solitary confinement? I will never know. It will always remain an enigma. An additional one…

Index

A
abandonment *37, 113, 131, 171*
abduction *16*
abuse *16, 70, 74, 123*
adulthood *155*
affection *98*
alienation *177–178*
Allende, Salvadore *19*
Altamirano, Carlos *24*
amenorrhoea *67*
anxiety *114, 127*
approval *92*
arbitrariness *24, 62, 70*
Arendt, Hannah *37, 58, 140*
Argentina *19*
arrest *20, 38*
assassination *16, 25, 72*
assembly *37*
association *37*
assurance *176*
asylum *89*
atrocities *96*
authoritarianism *32*
   colleagues *63*
autonomy *137, 174*

B
"bad moments" *49*
Bahía Blanca *187*
barbarity *180*
Beauvoir, Simone de *15, 170*
bedbugs *97*
belonging *39, 176*
Boards of Recognition *78, 92*
Bon Pasteur *41*
boredom *48, 61, 127*
bravery *81*
broken *172–173*
brutality *70*
Buenos Aires *19, 24, 27, 32, 91*

C
Cape Verde *31*
Castoriadis, Cornelius *140*
Catholicism *44, 177*
cell
   punishment cell *113, 127, 158*
certainty *178*
chaos *32, 158*
Charles de Gaulle Airport *169*
CIMADE *170*
class *49, 62*
claustrophobia *151*
cold *63, 73, 97, 111, 124*
   Cold War *20*
collaboration *87*

collectivity *103*
Comé, Joëlle *31, 179*
communications *55, 77, 86*
   coded communication *38*
   mental communication *40*
   sign language *77*
Communism *19, 21*
community *39*
companions *83*
concentration camp *16, 26, 32, 78, 103, 117, 119, 163, 172*
confidence *131, 160*
confinement *39*
confrontation *157*
confusion *66, 75, 153, 172*
convent *41*
cooking *61*
Córdoba *19*
corruption *44, 50*
counting *87*
coup d'état *19, 25*
courage *81*
Court of Appeals *22, 70*
cowardice *155*
crackdown *158*
criminal damage *109, 113*
criminalisation *21*
cruelty *70, 96, 115*

D

"dancing" *70*
death *81, 171*
   dead inside *170*
democracy *22, 163*
denial *31*

denunciation *20*
desolation *84, 129*
desperation/despair *39, 115, 144*
Devoto Prison *27, 91*
Diana *77*
dictatorship *15*
disappearance *15–16, 26, 106, 181*
discipline *61*
discrimination *160*
diversity *183*
divorce *175*
documentary *31*
dreams *172*
dysentery *39*

E

elimination *181*
embroidery *61*
emotion *62, 92, 103, 164*
escape *57, 187*
   escape plan *79*
estrangement *167*
exams *154*
exclusion *143*
exile *169, 183*
exploitation *19*
extermination *24*

F

family *19, 27, 43, 89, 143*
   cut off from seeing *70*
Fascism *108*
father *62, 101*
fatigue *113, 159*
fear *15, 71, 125, 127, 145, 169*

feelings *29, 63*
Ferrier, Christine *32, 179*
food *97, 109, 127*
fragility *155, 171*
France *15, 108, 169*
France Terre d'Asile *164*
freedom *21, 170, 174*
friendship *169*
Fringe *77, 109*
   separation from *92*

G

Gabon *31*
Galíndez, Jesús *109, 144, 153*
García, Prudencio *26*
Geneva *31, 171*
Giscard d'Estaing, Valéry *164*
guards *93, 158*
guerrillas *15, 54, 71, 157, 187*
Guevara, Che *57*
guilt *31, 60, 145*
gymnastics *70*

H

hair
   haircut *72*
   torn out *77*
harassment *84*
hardship *29, 113*
health. See also *mental health*
   medical care *146*
helplessness *31, 67*
High School Students Union *131*
hope *45, 140, 144*
hostages *187*

Hoz, José Martínez de *70, 187*
human and social contact *118*
human rights *15, 163, 170*
humiliation *68, 72, 74, 93*
hunger *63, 97, 128*
husband *38, 41, 65*
hygiene *97*

I

idealism *39*
identity *20, 46, 133, 138, 169, 176, 180*
imagination *132, 155*
imprisonment *15*
inequality *19*
integrity *46, 114, 121, 143*
International Committee of the Red Cross *144, 179*
interrogation *83*
isolation *16, 31, 37, 83, 137*
   internal isolation *110*
   political and ideological *103*
Italy *138*

J

Jewishness *163*
Jorge Newberry Airport *187*
justice *ix, 61, 98, 145*

K

kindness *98, 148*
knitting *43*
Kosovo *31*

L

Lager *143*

La Plata Prison *96*
laziness *61*
left, leftist, left-wing *15*
letters *30, 90, 96, 151*
Levi, Primo *172*
liberation *176*
literature *176*
loneliness *31, 37, 47, 91, 103, 169*
lucidity *92*

M

malaise *153*
Manuel Belgrano College *19*
Marx, Karl *19*
Mason, General Carlos *24*
melancholy *48, 185*
memory *ix, 40, 90, 101, 113, 171, 172, 179*
mental health *32, 74, 127*
    mental emptiness *128*
militancy *20*
military *15, 69*
missing persons *24*
Montoneros *54, 57, 79, 103, 159*
morale *41, 158*
morality *143*
Moravia, Alberto *176*
Moukarzel, José René *73*
murder *181*
music *61, 90, 157, 184*
    partisan songs *104*

N

naïvety *100*
National College of Commerce *20*
National Executive Power *25*

Nazism *37, 84, 172*
nervousness *127, 158*
nightmare *167*
nostalgia *179*
nothingness *28, 87, 124, 127, 137, 151, 173, 180*
nuns *41*

O

oppression *19, 75, 125, 178*
optimism *100*
otherness *139, 176*

P

Pablo *131, 180*
pain *16, 29, 92, 128, 143, 153*
    pain of exile *169*
paramilitaries *15, 45*
Paris *13–16, 28, 171, 183*
partisan songs *157*
passion *175*
passivity *81*
People's Revolutionary Army *54, 73, 96, 103, 177, 187*
Pérez, Corporal *74*
Peronismo de Base *103*
Perón, María Estela Martínez *15, 25, 38*
personality *174*
Piglia, Ricardo *24*
Plaza de Mayo *19*
poems *90*
Poland *172*
police *15, 27, 44, 53, 123*
political prisoners *55, 65, 109, 144*
Ponzio, Augusto *138*

poverty *19, 63*
power *58, 74, 109, 165*
  power cuts *80*
  powerlessness *37, 113, 145, 151, 173*
prayer *83*
Prete, Graciela Lo *59*
Primatesta, Cardinal *81*
prison *35–110, 46*
  showpiece prison *91*
privileges *160*
propaganda *22*
prostitutes *38*
psyche *140*
psychoanalysis *172*
psychological aspects *66, 90, 119*
psychology *32*
punishment
  punishment cell *33*

R

reading *61, 103, 176*
reality *55, 102, 129, 145, 169*
recognition *143*
Red Cross *31*. See also *International Committee of the Red Cross*
repression *15, 44, 60, 72, 157*
restrictive measures *65*
Rigatuso, Transito *180*
right, right-wing *15*
rights *22*
Río Cuarto *19, 41*
rupture *33*

S

sacrifice *178*

sadness *171, 185*
safety *131–132*
sanctions *16, 157*
Sarlo, Beatriz *24*
search *158*
sectarianism *157, 160*
security *16, 172*
  State security *21*
self-image *170*
sewing *61*
shadows *172*
shame *70, 155*
shooting *78*
silence *91, 129, 179*
  silencing *25*
  silent scream *113*
singing *158, 165, 184*
sisters *108*
social role *174*
solidarity *55, 169*
solitary confinement *16, 33, 143, 173*
solitude *65, 105, 129, 171*
sport *61*
stereotyping *62*
study *61, 154*
suffering *173, 176*
sweets *94*
Switzerland *28*

T

tears *30, 32, 115, 179, 185*
tensions *104, 115, 157*
terror *15, 37, 90, 157, 185*
testimony *31*
threats *45, 140*

torture *16, 31, 73, 123, 129, 178, 187*
totalitarian regimes *37*
transfer *78, 91*
trauma *29, 172*
trust *80*
truth *177, 178*
tunnel *81, 187*
tyranny *187*

U

uncertainty *169*
United Nations High Commission for Refugees *164, 169*
University of Bari *138*

V

Valium *148*
values *137, 174, 176, 184*
Vanguardia Comunista *19, 131*
Verhaeghe, Paul *172*
Videla, General Jorge *69, 187*
Vietnam *20*
violence *173*
visits *65, 99*
   deprivation of *157*
   visiting rooms *107*
void *118, 125, 165*
vulnerability *173*

W

whistling *38, 43*
World Cup *163*
wounds *180*
writing *61*

Other books from Waterside Press featuring political incarceration

The Maze Prison
A Hidden Story of Chaos, Anarchy and Politics
Tom Murtagh OBE
Foreword by Phillip Wheatley CB

Shows how an establishment built to hold those involved in terrorism, atrocities, murder and allied crimes became a pawn in The Troubles in Northern Ireland.

'A must read for those interested in the legacy of our troubled past'— The Rt Hon Sir Jeffrey Donaldson MP.

'I commend the book'— John Semple, Former Deputy Director of Operations, Northern Ireland Prison Service.

Hardback, paperback & ebook
ISBN 978-1-909976-50-4 | 2018 | 832 pages

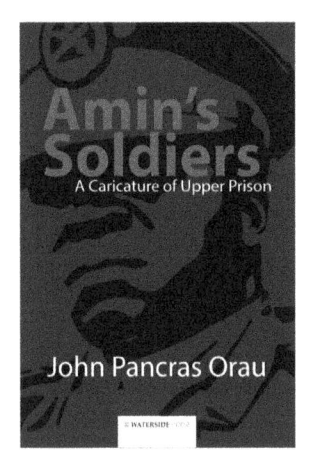

Amin's Soldiers
A Caricature of Upper Prison
John Pancras Orau

A book about crime and punishment in a highly-charged political landscape — about ordinary people whose only offence was to be left on the wrong side of history in Uganda. A true story of hope and belief, *Amin's Soldiers* is a masterpiece of tragicomic writing.

'A fascinating story, beautifully told, with episodes that are common to prisons the world over'— David Faulkner CB

Paperback & ebook
ISBN 978-1-904380-96-2 | 2013 | 200 pages

www.WatersidePress.co.uk